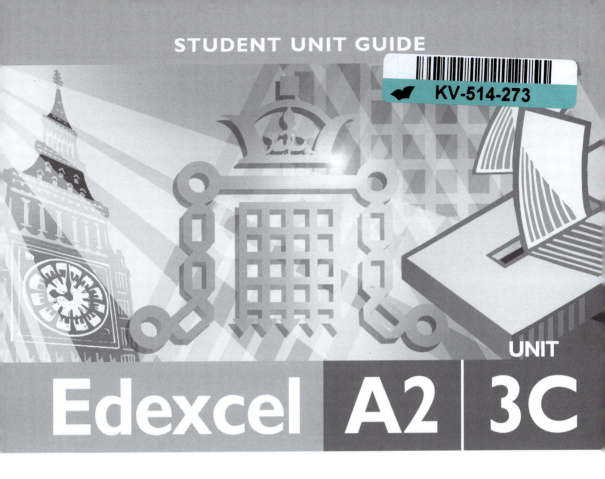

UNIT

Edexcel A2 | 3C

Government & Politics

Representative Processes in the USA

William Storey

Series Editor: Eric Magee

Philip Allan Updates, an imprint of Hodder Education, an Hachette UK company, Market Place, Deddington, Oxfordshire OX15 0SE

Orders

Bookpoint Ltd, 130 Milton Park, Abingdon, Oxfordshire OX14 4SB
tel: 01235 827720
fax: 01235 400454
e-mail: uk.orders@bookpoint.co.uk
Lines are open 9.00 a.m.–5.00 p.m., Monday to Saturday, with a 24-hour message answering service. You can also order through the Philip Allan Updates website: www.philipallan.co.uk

ISBN 978-0-340-98710-0

First printed 2009
Impression number 5 4 3 2 1
Year 2014 2013 2012 2011 2010 2009

This guide has been written specifically to support students preparing for the Edexcel A2 Government & Politics Unit 3C examination. The content has been neither approved nor endorsed by Edexcel and remains the sole responsibility of the author.

Typeset by Phoenix Photosetting, Chatham, Kent
Printed by MPG Books, Bodmin

Hachette UK's policy is to use papers that are natural, renewable and recyclable products and made from wood grown in sustainable forests. The logging and manufacturing processes are expected to conform to the environmental regulations of the country of origin.

Contents

Introduction

The specification at a glance.. 5

Skills you need to succeed 6

How to develop these skills.. 8

Testing these skills in exams.. 10

■ ■ ■

Content Guidance

About this section.. 14

Elections and voting

The electoral system 15

The nomination process 19

Elections.. 22

Direct democracy 27

Concerns about US electoral processes... 28

Conclusion.. 31

Pressure groups

Aims of pressure groups... 32

Access points 33

Influencing the federal government 34

Regulating pressure groups.. 42

The overall impact of pressure groups 42

Conclusion.. 44

Political parties

Umbrella parties... 45

Party realignment... 46

Democratic Party support 47

Republican Party support... 49

Party policies.. 50

Minor parties.. 52

Conclusion.. 54

A2 Government & Politics

Racial and ethnic politics

Racial inequality in the USA 55

Affirmative action 58

Conclusion 64

■ ■ ■

Questions and Answers

About this section 68

Question 1 Elections and voting 69

Question 2 Pressure groups 72

Question 3 Political parties 78

Question 4 Racial and ethnic politics 82

Introduction

This guide has been written to help you prepare more effectively for the Unit 3C Representative Processes in the USA examination for the Edexcel Advanced (A2) GCE in Government & Politics.

Its aim is to give a clear outline of the way in which the unit is structured and examined, as well as providing you with a summary of the content for each part of the unit. Unit 4C, Governing the USA, is covered in a separate unit guide.

The specification at a glance

The unit is divided into four areas, shown in the table below.

Topic	Content outline
Elections and voting	• How the electoral system works • Concerns about the electoral system • The outcome of recent elections
Pressure groups	• Why and how pressure groups exploit the political landscape • The impact of pressure groups, positive or negative, on the democratic system
Political parties	• What the main parties stand for: the main political ideas within each party • Patterns of support for each party • The role of minor parties
Race and ethnic politics	• The nature, extent and causes of racial inequality in the USA • Strategies for promoting greater racial equality

Freedom and opportunity

There is a theme running through these topics: US citizens judge the health of their political system by the extent to which it promotes freedom and opportunity.

The Statue of Liberty, once the gateway to the USA for immigrants arriving from Europe, bears an inscription: 'Give me your tired, your poor, your huddled masses yearning to breathe free...' What other country has ever invited strangers with little to offer and promised them a better life?

Nor is the Statue of Liberty the only US symbol that promises freedom and opportunity. The war that led to the USA's independence from Britain was launched with a proclamation that 'all men are created equal, that they are endowed by their Creator with certain unalienable rights, that among these are life, liberty and the pursuit of happiness', a sentiment that is celebrated and reinforced every year on 4 July. The national anthem, performed in a vast array of distinctive styles (and always with intensity and passion) at all major public events, culminates with the assertion that the USA is 'the land of the free and the home of the brave'.

Exclusion

Although American society, character and identity were shaped by the millions of hopeful migrants whose first sight of their new homeland was the Statue of Liberty, it was also shaped by the millions of men, women and children brought from Africa to a new world where freedom and opportunity would be actively and viciously denied.

Traded as if they were mere commodities, stripped of their identities by being punished if they spoke their native languages or lived according to their traditional cultures, and banned from learning to read and write, they were denied the freedom to live where they wanted, make the most of their abilities and create wealth that could provide a foundation for subsequent generations to build on. Even after the abolition of slavery, black Americans were forced by both custom and law to live outside mainstream America by a system that protected and reinforced white supremacy.

Politics

This combination of unrivalled opportunity for some and exclusion for others is found not only in America's history but also in each aspect of its politics. Do elections ensure effective representation for all? Do pressure groups help reinforce the dominance of the wealthy? Are political parties effective vehicles enabling different groups in a diverse nation to pursue their interests? To what extent do racial minorities enjoy true equality of opportunity?

If you can grasp how important these issues are in a country that bases its national identity on the principles of freedom and opportunity, explain the competing viewpoints on the political controversies that arise from these issues, and do so under the pressures of an exam, you will excel in this unit.

Skills you need to succeed

The A2 course helps you to build on the skills you developed at AS, while adding new skills that will be invaluable at university and throughout any working career.

Knowledge and understanding

The US political system is governed by a written constitution, which declares that its aims are to 'establish justice...promote the general welfare, and secure the blessings of liberty'. It is therefore important to understand how the system is *supposed* to work and how it *actually* works.

In addition to acquiring this body of knowledge, it is important that you learn and use the vocabulary of US politics, including the words and phrases that are unique to it (e.g. filibuster, affirmative action). You also need to be able to express yourself clearly, with precision and in concise terms by mastering the political language encountered at both AS and A2.

Application

At this academic level there will rarely be a time when it is appropriate for you to provide all the information you have. In response to all A2 political questions, you will be expected to apply your knowledge and understanding selectively, according to the issues you are being asked to address.

Analytical skills

You will be expected to explain a point of view effectively, even if you do not agree with it. Being able to understand all political perspectives and explain them, regardless of your personal opinions, is one of the most important skills you have to demonstrate in exams, and worthy of the highest marks.

Evaluation

You have to demonstrate the ability to weigh up the merits of competing viewpoints. Evaluation means much more than comparing the number of points that are made on two sides of an argument and deciding in favour of the one with the longer list. It means applying mature judgement to the quality and weight of those arguments. One opinion may be supported by a dozen valid points, all of which are weak or insubstantial. A rival opinion may be supported by just a few points that are far stronger or more substantial.

Synoptic skills

All the skills already outlined will help you to understand information and arguments, which can promote well-informed, thoughtful discussion. Such intense focus, however, can cause people to lose sight of the bigger picture.

In the final analysis, the study of US politics is about what the system is intended to achieve and whether it does so. Your ability to acquire knowledge, identify the most relevant aspects of that knowledge, analyse viewpoints on specific aspects of the political system and weigh up the strengths and weaknesses of those viewpoints is what will help you to reach and express useful conclusions about the US political system and its processes.

The A-level course, therefore, also promotes skills that ensure you keep the whole political system in mind when concentrating on any single aspect of that system.

This is known as the development of synoptic skills. For each aspect of the course that you are studying, you will be expected to demonstrate that you can do the following:

- **Identify viewpoints or perspectives.** In the case of US politics, this means establishing the extent to which each aspect of the Constitution serves to 'establish justice...promote the general welfare, and secure the blessings of liberty'. For example, do pressure groups in the USA tend to strengthen the position of those who already dominate society in terms of group numbers or wealth (not for the benefit of the 'general welfare') or, alternatively, do they tend to provide opportunities for everyone to be heard so that all groups may make a contribution to shaping their society?

- **Recognise the nature and extent of the rivalry between these viewpoints.** Continuing the example of pressure groups, those who argue that the US political system has provided freedom and opportunity for all tend to support the viewpoint that pressure groups play a constructive role in society. This argument is usually offered by people in the centre ground of US politics or those on the right of the political spectrum. Those on the left of US politics forcefully disagree, perceiving pressure groups as a significant factor in reinforcing inequality in US society, which they see as contrary to the spirit of the Constitution.

- **Demonstrate awareness of the importance of these viewpoints.** Not all issues are of equal significance, and students are expected to demonstrate that they recognise this. In the UK, there is a fascination with the Electoral College (the system for electing the president, in which each state is treated as a separate electoral contest). It has the potential to enable a candidate to win the presidency despite polling fewer votes than the opponent, as happened in the 2000 election, and there was animated discussion in the British press at the time about whether it should have been reformed or even abolished. However, it never became a major political issue in the USA, not least because its retention or abolition would make little difference to whether the US political system could be legitimately described as providing freedom and opportunity to all, which is the overriding political concern.

How to develop these skills

There is a range of learning strategies that will help you to do well at A-level.

Classroom learning

Lessons establish a foundation for learning and then steadily build on it. One strategy for success, therefore, is consistent lesson attendance. With all the demands of the final year at school or college (university open days, interviews, leadership responsibilities, coursework demands in other subjects etc.) or of fitting in a course around work and family, it can be all too easy to miss a few lessons.

However, one lesson missed in a week may be as much as a quarter of the classroom learning, and if that happens on three or four occasions over a term, a 'few' absences amount to having missed a week's learning in a congested academic year. The consequent gaps limit your ability to develop the detailed understanding of the US political system, and the range of viewpoints, needed to perform at the highest level.

Textbook learning

Given the depth of understanding required to achieve the highest grades at A-level, the work done in the classroom needs to be reinforced by reading a textbook. As a topic is being covered by your teacher, you should read the relevant sections of the textbook between lessons and, ideally, read it again as a whole once the topic has been completed.

This not only reinforces your understanding of the issues but also helps you to build the political vocabulary that you need in order to properly understand exam questions and to provide the kind of concise responses that are essential under the time pressure of exams. The structured approach of textbooks will also help you to develop the academic writing style used in the best essays.

Wider reading, listening and viewing

You are expected to have a sufficient level of awareness of current affairs to be able to discuss political issues in the light of any recent developments and to illustrate points you are making with relevant up-to-date examples.

UK newspapers

You can keep reasonably up to date by regularly reading the international section of UK newspapers such as *The Times*, the *Guardian*, the *Telegraph*, the *Independent* and the *Financial Times*.

Magazines

The US section of *The Economist* is an excellent resource for US politics. The final article in this section, 'Lexington', always offers a viewpoint on an aspect of US politics that helps to develop the analytical, evaluative and synoptic skills outlined above.

US newspapers

The two prestigious 'newspapers of record' in the USA, the *New York Times* and the *Washington Post*, have online editions with the latest US political news. If you subscribe (which you can do free of charge), the headlines will be sent to you by e-mail each day and you can scroll down, see which stories look promising, and click on those you wish to read. Then you can either retain or delete the e-mail. This is an excellent way of keeping up to date.

Television and radio

The programmes that should have become a standard feature of life while you were studying AS politics, *Channel 4 News*, BBC2's *Newsnight* and BBC Radio 4's *Today Programme* and *PM*, are also valuable resources for US politics at A2. Additionally, anyone with access to the internet would benefit from tuning in to NPR (National Public Radio, the US equivalent of the BBC), which manages to combine thoughtful, in-depth news coverage with a calming, relaxed atmosphere. Some digital television stations also screen late-night talk shows from the USA that provide light-hearted but informative commentary on the latest political developments, for example *The Daily Show* on More4.

US political websites

All the main US news organisations have websites that provide political coverage and background material. There are also sites dedicated entirely to politics, such as *Real Clear Politics*, that bring together news articles and commentaries from (mainly right-wing) newspapers across the USA; sites dedicated to an aspect of US politics, such as *270towin*, that focus on presidential elections; and blogs such as *Daily Kos* that provide a forum for left-wing political activists. Most textbooks guide students towards the best websites for each topic as they are being studied.

Testing these skills in exams

The knowledge and academic skills of students are tested in written examinations. There is no coursework.

The Unit 3 examination can be taken in either January or June.

The examination will always include questions on all four topics:
- Elections and voting
- Pressure groups
- Political parties
- Racial and ethnic politics

The examination lasts for 1 hour 30 minutes. In that time, you will have to respond to two types of question: short-answer questions and essay questions.

Short-answer questions

Each answer is worth 15 marks and should take about 15 minutes to complete. There will be five of these questions in Section A of the exam, and you will have to choose *three* of them to answer.

Knowledge and understanding

In each of these questions, the examiner will be considering the quality of your knowledge and understanding of the key feature of US politics that is at the heart of the question. So if we take an example from the sample material published by the exam board — 'How significant are mid-term elections?' — the key feature is the congressional elections that take place halfway through a presidential term of office. You would be expected to demonstrate that you know that all 435 members of the House of Representatives face re-election, having served just a 2-year term, and a third of all Senators also face re-election having served 6-year terms.

Analysis and evaluation

The examiner will also be considering the quality of your analysis and evaluation. Thus, in the case of the question on mid-term elections, you would be expected to demonstrate the ability to explain (analyse) the factors that should be considered when judging the importance of these elections — both the points that suggest they are not significant and the points that suggest they matter a great deal. You would also be expected to demonstrate the ability to *weigh up* (evaluate) the significance of those factors — which are more substantial and which are comparatively trivial.

It may be that you explain three points which suggest that mid-term elections do not have a substantial impact (e.g. low turnout, local factors determining most outcomes, high rates of incumbents being re-elected) and only two points suggesting that they are of significance (e.g. the standing and authority of the president being affected if his party performs either very well or quite poorly; the factors affecting the outcome of the mid-terms playing a role in shaping the tactics and strategies in the subsequent presidential election), but that these two points are weightier than the three suggesting that mid-terms are not particularly important. If it appears to the examiner that you are simply listing points but not applying maturity of judgement to them (e.g. your conclusion is that three points outweigh two simply because there are more of them), you will not be awarded many marks for the quality of your analysis and evaluation.

Linking

Examiners expect you to be able to link these skills together, demonstrating an ability to construct and communicate coherent arguments, making use of a range of appropriate vocabulary and examples in one articulate response. If you produce a three-paragraph answer, with one paragraph that provides evidence of knowledge and understanding, one that provides evidence of analysis and one that provides evidence of evaluation, the examiner is not likely to be impressed. Politics is not like chemistry, where you can put first one ingredient in a test tube, then another, then a third, and step back to watch as it miraculously combines to produce an entirely new substance. It is more like a piece of artwork, in which a picture in a person's mind emerges and takes shape on a blank sheet. The artist may have used a variety of skills but it is not these, individually, that are admired. Rather it is the ways in which they have been combined to produce art that is both technically accomplished and thought-provoking. Similarly, the best responses to short-answer questions use analytical and evaluative skills to build seamlessly to a conclusion.

Examples of how this is done well, and not so well, are found in the Questions and Answers section of this guide.

Essay questions

There will be three essay questions in Section B of the exam, and you have to choose *one* of them to answer. This is worth 45 marks and should take about 45 minutes to complete.

Developing an argument

Although examiners will be looking for the skills outlined above, far more is required in an essay than in a short-answer question. In the additional time available, you are expected to develop an argument in response to the question. This means:

- **deciding** your answer to the question
- **persuading** the reader of the merits of your case by presenting the arguments that support your conclusion
- **explaining** why this viewpoint is contested, by outlining the counter-argument (which will inevitably include acknowledging the weaknesses in the argument you have made)
- **defending** your viewpoint by arguing that the counter-arguments are outweighed by the case you are making, even when the weaknesses of your viewpoint are taken into account

In this exercise, you are doing far more than putting forward two points of view ('some say this, while others say that') and evaluating the strengths of the two arguments in your conclusion. You are developing a case that one set of arguments (note: these are academic arguments, not personal opinions) is stronger than a rival set of arguments and, in doing so, evaluating points of view throughout your essay.

Synoptic skills

It is essential to show evidence of synoptic skills, which are defined as identification of differing viewpoints or perspectives, and an awareness of how these viewpoints affect the interpretation of political events or issues and shape the conclusions drawn.

Examples of how this is done well, and not so well, are also found in the Questions and Answers section of this guide.

Content
Guidance

This section provides you with a concise overview of the knowledge needed for this unit. The topics covered are:

- Elections and voting
- Pressure groups
- Political parties
- Racial and ethnic politics

More importantly, it examines the various debates that arise from the way the US political system operates and the rival points of view. In many cases, there are just two viewpoints, criticising or defending aspects of the political processes covered in this unit, but in some cases there is a range of opinions — or there are groups that share the same objective but for different reasons.

Above all, this section sets these debates in the wider context of the overall aims of the Founding Fathers when they designed the political framework of the USA, to promote freedom and equality of opportunity by keeping politicians in check. Accordingly, this section provides you with the means to develop an effective argument in response to questions requiring you to reach a reasoned conclusion about the extent to which each aspect of the US political system contributes towards, or hinders, fulfilment of the Founding Fathers' objectives.

Elections and voting

For the Founding Fathers, power was dangerous. Whether in the hands of an individual or of a group, it represented a threat to liberty and opportunity. The greater the power, the greater the threat. That is why the Constitution is designed to limit the amount of power any one person (or group) can wield: federalism, separation of powers, checks and balances are all designed to fragment political power.

Elections are also supposed to be a check on power and prevent the abuse of power. Once elected, politicians should be acutely aware that they serve the interests of the people and will be held accountable by the people — and thrown out of office — if they are incompetent or misuse their powers. Additionally, in some states citizens have the opportunity to bypass politicians whom they believe are insensitive to their concerns by getting their own proposals for changes to the law added to the ballot papers.

Many Americans, however, are not convinced that the electoral processes achieve the goal of maintaining a check on power. There is a widespread belief that the wealthier sections of society (often contemptuously referred to as 'special interests') have devised ways of using the electoral process for their own gain, to the disadvantage of the middle class and especially the poor, and that it does not effectively serve to hold politicians to account. A substantial number of US citizens are so cynical about the electoral system, so sure that they cannot make a difference, that they do not even vote.

This section takes you through the various stages of the electoral process and provides you with the means to weigh up how effectively the electoral system achieves the goal of ensuring that politicians serve the best interests of their constituents, or whether they are captive to 'special interests'.

The electoral system

The USA uses the first-past-the-post electoral system for all federal elections. In each contest, whoever wins the most votes is elected.

All federal elections are also held on fixed dates, so that those in power cannot call an election when the political circumstances are favourable to them in order to extend their period in office.

There are three types of federal election — two for the legislature and one for the executive:

- The legislature, Congress, consists of two chambers: the House of Representatives and the Senate. All members of both chambers are elected, but they have separate electoral processes.

- The executive is also elected, in the person of the president, through an electoral process that is separate from the two sets of congressional elections.

The House of Representatives

The Founding Fathers made the House of Representatives responsible for decisions on how much tax to raise and how to spend it. As this was seen as having the greatest potential for corruption, and the most significant impact on ordinary people if the economy were mismanaged, they gave members of the House of Representatives short terms of office so that they could be frequently held to account. Members of the House of Representatives (confusingly known as Congressmen) serve 2-year terms of office. There is no limit to the number of times a Congressman can be re-elected.

The country is divided into 435 congressional districts, each returning one person to serve the interests of their area in the law-making process in Washington, DC. The number of congressional districts was fixed at 435 by a law passed in 1929. However, the population of America does not remain static — it grows and people move from one state to another. So, every 10 years, after the census that measures the size and distribution of the population, the district boundaries are redrawn to reflect changes since the previous census and to keep the number of voters in each district roughly equal.

The Senate

The Founding Fathers made the Senate responsible for protecting the interests of the states — especially the states with small populations, whose interests could potentially be overwhelmed in the House of Representatives, where they will always be outnumbered. Each state therefore has two members in the Senate, regardless of their size or population, making 100 in total since the USA grew to 50 states in 1958. Members of the Senate (helpfully known as Senators) serve 6-year terms of office. As with Congressmen, there is no limit to the number of times a Senator can be re-elected — Senator Byrd of West Virginia, the longest-serving Senator, was first elected in 1959.

Senators are not all elected at the same time, however. Every 2 years (at the same time as all 435 members of the House of Representatives face re-election), one-third of the Senators face re-election. This ensures that there is never a time when all members of the legislature are elected simultaneously, and therefore reduces the risk of one party sweeping to power at a time when political circumstances may have made one party extremely popular or the other extremely unpopular.

The president

The Founding Fathers gave the president, who is elected with a running-mate who becomes vice-president, a 4-year term of office. As with people elected to both chambers of the legislature, the Founding Fathers did not place a limit on the number of times that a president could be re-elected. However, after the first president, George Washington, voluntarily stepped down after being elected twice, it became generally accepted that if two terms in office were enough for the greatest American, that was all anyone would serve in the White House. When President Franklin D. Roosevelt disregarded this convention and was elected four times in the 1930s and 1940s, the Constitution was amended: now all presidents are limited to two terms.

Presidential elections are, in effect, 51 separate elections that are held on the same day to choose two people — one to run the country and another to take over if anything should happen to the president. The winning team (known as the presidential 'ticket') needs to win a majority of an Electoral College. Each state, plus the District of Columbia, has a certain number of Electoral College votes, related to the size of its population. Each state must have a minimum of 3 Electoral College votes, however small its population. California, which has the largest population, has 55 Electoral College votes. There are 538 electoral votes in total, so 270 votes are needed to win the presidency.

Whichever ticket wins the majority of votes in a state wins all the Electoral College votes of that state (with the exception of Maine and Nebraska, which allocate their Electoral College votes proportionately). The Electoral College votes of all the states are then tallied, and the ticket that crosses the 270-vote threshold is declared the winner.

The table below summarises the federal electoral system:

	Number	Term	Method of election	Term limits?
President and vice-president	2	4 years	Winner of the Electoral College — first to 270 votes	Yes: two 4-year terms
House of Representatives	435	2 years	First past the post — winner of a district (that may be redrawn or eliminated after the census)	No
Senate	100	6 years	First past the post — winner of a state	No

First past the post

The first-past-the-post electoral system has several disadvantages that will be familiar to anyone who has studied British politics, including the following:
- Small parties without concentrated support have little chance of electoral success.
- All the votes cast for any candidate other than the winner are effectively wasted.
- This system encourages tactical voting, with people voting against the candidate they dislike the most, because their preferred candidate has no realistic chance of winning.
- It also reduces participation in elections, as some people prefer not to vote at all if there is no chance of their preferred candidate winning.

- Additionally, parties hardly campaign in areas where they cannot win or where they know they will win even if they do not court the voters.
- If there are multiple candidates standing, the overall winner may have less than half of the votes cast, meaning that the majority of voters would have preferred another representative.

Electoral College

The Electoral College system, as used in the USA, magnifies some of these disadvantages in the following ways:

- It is almost impossible to break the stranglehold of the Democrats and Republicans on the Electoral College. This was demonstrated in 1992, when Ross Perot, a billionaire who funded his own campaign, struck a chord with the American people. He based his campaign on the argument that the budget deficit was the greatest challenge facing the country and the main parties were doing the people a disservice by not addressing it. He polled 18.9% of the overall vote, but because he did not come first in any state he did not win any Electoral College votes.
- Tactical voting becomes even more important than in other elections. In the 2000 presidential election, the Green Party candidate, Ralph Nader, won only 2.7% of the vote but, crucially, he polled 97,000 votes in the key state of Florida, which George W. Bush won by just 537 votes — meaning that the Green supporters effectively handed victory to the presidential candidate with the worst programme on the environment from their point of view. Not surprisingly, when Nader ran again in 2004, his share of the vote fell to 0.34%.
- The candidates put all their efforts into wooing the voters in those states that both parties have a realistic chance of winning — known as 'swing' or 'battleground' states. In recent elections, candidates have put a disproportionate amount of time and resources into swing states with a large number of Electoral College votes, especially Florida (27 votes), Ohio (20 votes) and Pennsylvania (21 votes). This in turn has the effect of depressing turnout in the other states. Why bother to vote when the outcome is virtually certain?
- It is possible, even likely, that a candidate will become president (through the votes of the Electoral College) without winning over 50% of the popular vote. President Clinton was elected twice with 43% and 49.2% of the vote (with Ross Perot running strong third-party campaigns both times); President George W. Bush was elected with half a million fewer votes than his rival, Al Gore, in 2000 because he won safe Republican states and swing states by modest margins while the Democrat piled up huge numbers of 'wasted' votes in safe Democratic states but fared badly elsewhere.
- It is hard for small, extreme parties to gain the credibility that comes from participation in the federal branches of government.

Advantages

First past the post and the Electoral College also have significant advantages, however:

- These systems offer simplicity and speed. They are more straightforward, and easier to understand, than many other electoral systems. The counting of ballot papers in a first-past-the-post election should also be swift, with the outcome known within hours of the polling stations closing.
- One of the two main parties always wins a majority in the House of Representatives, one always has a majority in the Senate, and one captures the White House. As the same party may not control all three institutions, they may have to compromise, but this is still a clearer and more transparent arrangement than the multi-party coalitions that result from some other electoral systems.
- The Electoral College forces presidential candidates to consider the interests of most sections of the population.
- Also, the Electoral College forces candidates to court the vote of the smaller states that could well be overlooked if the result were based on simply tallying the popular vote.

The nomination process

For the voters, the electoral process starts well before the election that determines who will take office in Washington, DC. This is because US voters, unlike those in most other countries, have a say in who represents each party in the election.

Primaries

Before an election for the House of Representatives or the Senate, there will be an opportunity for people to put themselves forward as the best person to represent one of the two main parties and appeal to the voters to select them. These contests are called primaries. The rules and timing of primaries vary from state to state.

The nomination for presidential elections is a lengthy affair. The candidates for each party compete in primaries, state by state, starting in January of election year and ending in June. The value of winning the primary is related to the population of each state. The candidate who wins the most votes in a state gains the support of its delegates at the national convention in the summer, with heavily populated states having more delegates than lightly populated states. When one candidate has won more than half of all the delegates, he or she has effectively won — although formal victory is not declared until the national convention takes place.

In practice, once it becomes clear to the other contestants that one of the candidates is pulling ahead of the rest, they start withdrawing from the race: thus the outcome can often be determined before most of the primaries take place. On the rare occasions when there is a close contest between the two leading candidates, it may continue until the last primary. This is what happened in the 2008 Democratic primaries, with Hillary Clinton not conceding victory until 4 days after the final primary in June 2008.

Open primaries

Some states hold open primaries, in which <u>any registered voter can participate.</u> On the day of the election, voters can decide if they want to cast their ballot in the Democratic or Republican contest, but they cannot vote in both. This enables <u>independent voters</u> to take part in the nomination process, boosting overall partici- pation, but it also provides an opportunity for committed supporters of one party to '<u>raid</u>' the other party's contest, voting for the weakest candidate in the hope of boosting their own party's chances once the candidates have been chosen.

Closed primaries

Other states hold closed primaries. <u>Only voters registered as supporters of a party can participate in their party's primary.</u> While this limits the number of voters able to participate, it ensures that the party's candidate is chosen by people with a commit- ment to the interests of the party and, possibly, a greater level of political awareness.

Caucuses

Some states, usually those with a large geographical area but a small population, hold caucuses instead of primaries. These are a <u>series of open meetings,</u> typically lasting <u>2–3 hours,</u> in which the <u>participants attempt to persuade each other to support their preferred candidate before a vote is held.</u> The candidate who wins the most votes across the state wins the caucus. These contests require an even greater level of commitment and political knowledge than closed primaries, but have the lowest level of participation and are best suited to the types of community where people are comfortable hosting strangers in their homes or community centres.

Advantages

Overall, the US nomination process has much to commend it, for the following reasons:

- <u>It stops politicians in safe seats becoming lazy and complacent.</u>
- It enables <u>ordinary people to participate</u> in the democratic process.
- It provides an <u>opportunity for rival policies to be aired and tested</u> with the electorate before the election. In presidential elections, it also tests the <u>mettle of the candidates.</u> <u>Barack Obama</u>, who had won his Senate seat comfortably when the campaign of his Republican opponent collapsed in scandal, demonstrated the extent of his character and purpose for the first time during the primary campaign. In contrast, the campaigns of two of the Republican candidates in 2008, Rudy Giuliani and Fred Thompson, faltered because of a perception that they found campaigning across the country too gruelling.
- Above all, <u>it gives candidates who would have little chance of being selected by party leaders (insurgents) a genuine opportunity of running for office</u> in one of the main parties. This has been true of the last three Democratic presidents. Jimmy <u>Carter, Bill Clinton and Barack Obama</u> all started their campaigns as little-known outsiders, but each fired the imagination of the electorate and came through to win.

content guidance

Disadvantages

However, this type of nominating process has been criticised in a number of ways:

- Candidates have to fund their own primary campaigns. To have a realistic chance of winning, candidates have to raise large sums of money, and as new campaign platforms such as the internet emerge, the need for money grows. In the case of presidential elections, with candidates campaigning across the country, the cost is magnified many times. In 2007–08, Hillary Clinton and Barack Obama each raised over $150 million. This level of finance makes it almost impossible to run for federal office unless a candidate has the wealth to fund his or her own campaign or connections to wealthy people who can donate to it.
- The contest between candidates can get bitter, leading to a publicly divided party that is weakened by the time of the election.
- The process has the potential to select an unsuitable candidate. Concern about this led the Democratic Party to modify its nomination process in 1980, giving votes to 'superdelegates' — Democrats elected to high office (e.g. Senators, Governors etc.) and senior party officials. In 2008, with neither of the leading contenders, Barack Obama and Hillary Clinton, able to deliver a knockout blow during the primaries, the superdelegate system was tested for the first time. Most, however, made it clear that they would follow, not challenge, the popular vote for fear of appearing undemocratic. Thus, although Hillary Clinton tried to persuade them to support her on the basis of her greater political experience, the majority of superdelegates backed the candidate with the lead at the end of the primaries, thereby sealing the nomination for the less experienced candidate, Barack Obama.

The table below summarises the nomination process:

Nomination system	Advantages	Disadvantages
Primaries	An opportunity for ordinary people to participate in the democratic process Prevents politicians in safe seats becoming lazy and complacent Gives insurgents an opportunity of being selected Rival policies to be aired and tested to increase electoral appeal	Cost of campaigns Contests can get bitter, weakening party Some candidates campaign on their personal qualities rather than policy Voters may make a less informed decision than party leaders
Open primaries Held in some states for the presidential election and for elections to the House of Representatives and the Senate	Higher participation, including independent voters	'Raiding' the other party's contest, to elect a weak candidate

Nomination system	Advantages	Disadvantages
Closed primaries Held in some states for the presidential election and for elections to the House of Representatives and the Senate	Higher commitment to the party and, possibly, a greater level of political awareness in comparison with open primaries	Lower participation in comparison with open primaries
Caucuses Held in some states, typically those with a large geographical area but small population	Higher commitment to the party and a greater level of political awareness in comparison with all primaries	Lower participation in comparison with all primaries

Elections

The general election

In congressional races there is usually a quiet period between the end of the nomination phase of the election, which normally takes place in the spring or early summer, and the start of the general election campaign between the two parties, which commences after Labor Day, the public holiday at the beginning of September.

National convention

In presidential races, these two phases of the campaign are bridged by each party holding a national convention. The national convention has a number of benefits for each party:

- It is an opportunity to heal wounds and demonstrate unity to the wider pubic. This was seen in the 2008 Democratic national convention in Denver, Colorado, following the increasingly bitter battle between Barack Obama and Hillary Clinton for the nomination.
- It brings together party activists from across the country.
- It enables the party's candidate to establishing a 'narrative' for the election campaign. For example, in 2004 the Republican convention effectively created a sense that voters faced a choice between a strong, decisive war leader (President Bush) and a 'flip-flopper' who lacked the clear, purposeful leadership skills needed at a time of national crisis (Senator Kerry).
- It may serve to provide a 'bounce' in the polls in the lead-in to the autumn campaign.

Despite these advantages, the national conventions have clearly been declining in significance. Before both parties adopted primaries to select their candidates in the 1970s, the convention was used by party leaders to choose their nominees for president and vice-president and to set out their policies (the 'platform') for the election. With so much at stake, the main television networks would provide a week of uninterrupted coverage of each convention. In recent election campaigns, however, as fewer important decisions have been made at the conventions, the networks have been steadily cutting back on their coverage. Also, while traditionally each party did not campaign during the other's national convention, this was not respected in 2008, and both candidates campaigned through each other's conventions.

Message

Once the campaign gets fully underway, the candidates for the major parties face two challenges.

The first is crafting an appealing message to the widest possible cross-section of the electorate. The candidates are appealing mainly to the most active, committed party supporters during the primaries, so they may need to modify their campaign themes to appeal to a wider range of voters before the general election. Barack Obama built his primary campaign on his early opposition to the Iraq war but, strikingly, immediately after securing the presidential nomination in the summer of 2008 he announced he would have to 'refine' his position on the war and adopted centrist stances on a number of issues, including support for a Supreme Court decision that weakened gun-control legislation.

The second challenge is conveying that message as effectively as possible. There are three strategies for communicating campaign messages, each described in terms of a military operation.

The ground war

Candidates depend heavily on support in each locality, with as many volunteers as possible helping likely supporters to register to vote if they have not yet done so, distributing campaign literature, phoning voters and knocking on doors to persuade them to support their candidate, helping supporters to fill in ballot papers and providing aid to supporters who have difficulty getting to a polling station — especially the elderly and people with disabilities. This operation is often more effective if the campaign is able to provide full-time paid organisers who can improve the profes- sionalism of the local effort. In 2008, Barack Obama set up more than three times as many field offices as John McCain.

In key marginal areas, the candidates add to the effort by campaigning in person, attending high-profile events and holding rallies. For example, in late October 2008, an Obama rally in the swing state of Colorado was attended by more than 150,000 people: a week later, polls indicated that he had built an 8% lead over his opponent.

The air war

Candidates can reach far more people, far more often, through television and radio than they can through their volunteers. A major factor in US elections, therefore, is the effectiveness of campaign advertisements, where they are broadcast and how often they are aired. This in turn depends in large measure on how much money candidates have been able to raise. In 2008, the Democratic candidate outspent his Republican opponent by a third in the final weeks of the campaign, culminating in the purchase of half an hour of primetime television on three of the four main networks (plus some cable channels) to broadcast an 'infomercial' that set out who he aimed to help as president and how he intended to achieve his aims. It was watched by over 34 million people and was the main focus of political discussion the following day.

The media can also play a significant role in the air war. In the USA, at both congressional and presidential level, it has become customary for candidates to have formal televised debates during the general election campaign. Although watched by millions of Americans — over 50 million watched the first debate between Barack Obama and John McCain in 2008 — they have rarely proved decisive. In most campaigns, including 2008, no candidate has been able to use the debates to deliver a knockout blow to an opponent. In 2008, the media's most significant impact occurred during a routine interview, in which the Republican vice-presidential candidate Sarah Palin was unable to provide satisfactory responses to straightforward questions. This confirmed the concern held by many, including independent voters in key states, that she was not qualified to be 'a heartbeat away from the presidency', especially when playing a supporting role to a man who would have been the oldest ever to take office for a first presidential term.

The cyberspace war

In the twenty-first century, the internet has become an increasingly important battle-ground. In 2004, Democratic presidential candidate Howard Dean attracted unexpected support through his website from people who had never previously been involved in politics but shared his opposition to the war in Iraq. A similar process resulted in the primary defeat of Senator Joe Lieberman in 2006. The Barack Obama campaign continued this trend, with the most extensive use of the internet yet seen. About half of the campaign's donations were made on its website. The site also provided a forum for people to meet other supporters, organise their activities and purchase merchandise. Unprecedented numbers of volunteers were recruited through the website. For example, when the campaign began setting up its operation in Texas (ahead of the primary), over 125,000 people had already signed up as volunteers. The website was also used as a means of direct communication, encouraging supporters to help spread the message. Thus when Barack Obama found himself embroiled in a controversy surrounding his pastor, Jeremiah Wright, his campaign sent an e-mail to all supporters with a link to the video of the 37-minute speech he had delivered in response. It was viewed in its entirely on YouTube over 5.2 million times, offsetting the media's negative coverage of the issue.

Voting

Finally, in the last 2 weeks of the campaign, voting begins — with 30 states allowing people a postal ballot without them having to give a reason and opening polling stations so that people can vote early.

This is in response to the complexity of ballot papers. As well as voting in federal elections, Americans vote in state and local elections and often on specific political proposals. In 2008, for example, a measure to ban gay marriage was almost as prominent in California as the presidential campaign.

One effect of such lengthy, complicated ballots, combined with voting regulations that vary from state to state (and sometimes from one area to another within a state), is that disputes surrounding the outcome are commonplace. An extreme case was the dispute about the outcome of the Electoral College vote in Florida in 2000, which meant that the presidential election was not finally determined until over a month after the election.

Once an election is finally over, the successful politicians take up their positions the following January. Even before that happens, however, the race for the next election may begin. In 2008, the presidential election took place on 4 November. Less than a week later, Republican Mike Huckabee signalled his intention to run in the 2012 presidential election.

Congressional elections

Elections for the House of Representatives and the Senate have a somewhat different character to presidential elections. The candidates are not running for national office: they are campaigning to represent the interests of their district (in the case of the House of Representatives) or their state (in the case of the Senate). The issues at the heart of these campaigns tend, therefore, to be about local matters. Candidates emphasise their determination to win the maximum share of federal resources for their area and to defend the interests of the locality — whether it be to protect the landscape or to support the main source of employment. Those running for re-election (incumbents) publicise all they have achieved for their area since the last election, while challengers often suggest that the incumbent has been seduced by the high life in Washington, DC and has lost touch with the concerns of ordinary people. This line of argument can be particularly effective in areas far away from the capital, where the work and lifestyles of federal politicians seem remote. However, incumbents usually guard against such attacks by frequently visiting their constituents, ensuring that their staff address any concerns raised by their voters and making sure they are seen attending important local events. These activities, combined with the federal resources secured for the area (e.g. a new high-tech research facility providing well-paid employment), result in a high percentage of incumbents being re-elected.

Incumbency advantage

Incumbent members of Congress generally find it easier to raise election campaign funds than their opponents do. Donors, especially those who hope to have some influence after the election, prefer to back a winner. Also, it is becoming increasingly common for the constituency boundaries of House of Representative seats to be redrawn in such a way as to ensure that a majority of the voters in the district are reliable supporters of the sitting representative's party. These additional hurdles to potential opponents deter challenges, and quite frequently incumbents, especially those in the House of Representatives, run unopposed. This is known as 'incumbency advantage'.

The incumbency-advantage effect is less pronounced in Senate election contests. This is partly because the candidates are campaigning to represent a state, and the boundaries for these elections do not change. More importantly, Senate contests tend to attract people from outside the world of politics who have funds and a profile to match those of the incumbent. For example, when Hillary Clinton ran for the Senate in 2000 she was already famous and had no difficulty raising donations.

Mid-term elections

Since the early 1990s, a new factor has played an increasingly important role in congressional elections, with a tendency to offset the incumbency-advantage effect. On several occasions, national factors have proved more significant than local issues. This trend has been particularly marked in mid-term elections, which take place 2 years after a presidential election:

- In 1994, 2 years after Bill Clinton won the presidency, candidates for the Republican Party ran on a platform called 'Contract with America'. This was a highly conservative package of proposals, targeted at the whole country, which aimed to capitalise on a perception that the president was adopting policies that were too left wing for most Americans. It was extremely successful and resulted in the Republicans winning a majority of seats in the House of Representatives.
- In 2002, in the aftermath of the 11 September 2001 attacks, the Republican Party campaigned across the country with a message that the president needed wholehearted support from Congress, which strongly implied that a vote for the Democratic Party was an act of disloyalty. This tactic proved highly effective, with the Republicans extending their majority in the House of Representatives and winning a majority of seats in the Senate.
- In 2006, with the reputation of President George W. Bush damaged by the poor handling of a major hurricane that had hit New Orleans, the war in Iraq going badly and members of the Republican Party having been embroiled in a series of scandals, the Democrats ran a national campaign arguing that a change of leadership was needed in Congress. As a result, the Democrats won control of both the House of Representatives and the Senate.

Mid-term elections have proved significant because of the effect they have had on presidents. Bill Clinton had to adopt a more centrist, at times even conservative, approach to policy after 1994. George W. Bush could usually rely on strong support from Congress after 2002: he vetoed only one bill over the following 4 years until his party lost control of both houses. After 2006, however, he vetoed 11 bills passed by the Democrat-controlled Congress.

The mid-term elections have also proved significant because they set the tone for the subsequent presidential campaign. With the 2002 mid-term campaign proving divisive, but effective for the Republican Party, when President George W. Bush ran for re-election in 2004 his campaign team adopted a similar approach. They made no attempt to win the support of Democrats or independents but concentrated on appealing to committed Republicans, especially those who had not voted 4 years earlier when George W. Bush had been more moderate in tone. The additional votes he won as a result secured him a second term. Similarly, with the message of change proving so effective for the Democrats in the 2006 mid-terms, it became the central theme of the campaign that won Barack Obama the presidential election 2 years later.

Direct democracy

Americans taking part in elections vote for candidates seeking office, but they may also have an opportunity to vote on a range of other issues in what are known as ballot measures. These take a variety of forms:

- referendums
- initiatives/propositions
- recalls

These measures are designed to enable the electorate to reinforce the legitimacy of decisions taken by elected politicians (referendums), to bypass professional politicians in order to secure legislation that they have failed to adopt (initiatives/propositions), or to force politicians out of office for reasons of incompetence or corruption (recalls).

They are not available in all states and they take different forms across the country, but where they are used they provide an opportunity for citizens to play a direct role in the political process. However, in common with all other electoral processes, they can cause concern about ways in which they may be misused.

Referendums, which are used in 24 states, provide voters with an opportunity to accept or reject a law passed by the state legislature.

Initiatives, used in 23 states and Washington, DC, provide voters with an opportunity to vote on issues that have not been addressed by the state legislature but which groups of voters feel strongly about. Initiatives are also known as propositions, because they consist of a proposal which is added to the ballot paper. The rules for putting an initiative on the ballot vary, with different states requiring that it have the support of anything from 5% to 15% of the electorate. If it is approved, winning a majority of the vote, it becomes law.

Recalls, used in 26 states, are an opportunity for voters to agree to the removal of a politician from office before his or her term has ended. In most cases, this is done because of a perception that the politician is not providing an adequate service to the community. Occasionally it will be used when a politician has been accused of corruption: usually this is dealt with by the state legislature through a process called impeachment, but if it is widely believed that the corrupt politician is being shielded by his or her colleagues, a recall election may result. Before the vote is held, signatures of registered voters (usually equal to 25% of votes cast in the previous election) have to be collected and verified. Then the voters can cast two votes — one to decide whether the politician should be removed from office, or 'recalled', and the second to choose the replacement. If there are not enough votes to secure the recall of the politician, he or she remains in office. If the majority of the electorate votes to remove the politician from office, the second votes are counted and the winning candidate then serves the remainder of the term of office.

These measures are part of the system known as direct democracy, which has a number of advantages:
- It gives people a direct say in decisions which affect them.
- It serves as an additional check on government and should make politicians less likely to abuse their powers.
- It helps to maintain a high level of interest in the political system. Even in presidential election years, campaigns on ballot measures have a high profile.
- Discussion of the issues brought to the fore by ballot measures serves to educate the electorate.
- Some politicians are better at campaigning than at governing. Recall elections provide the electorate with a method of removing politicians who impressed them during an election campaign but did not impress them in office.

Direct democracy also has a number of disadvantages, however:
- Many ballot measures are initiated not by groups of ordinary citizens but by well-organised, well-funded special interests.
- Direct democracy may restrict the ability of elected representatives to do their job. In California, for example, since the success of Proposition 13 in 1978, the state legislature has not been able to raise property taxes to fund services, which puts a disproportionate burden on taxpayers who are not homeowners.
- Direct democracy tends to work to the disadvantage of minority and poor groups that are unable to muster the number of votes or funds needed to defend their interests.

Concerns about US electoral processes

Why are there widespread concerns in the USA that elections do not effectively hold politicians to account, and are manipulated by wealthier sections of society for their own gain?

Cost

The funding of campaigns has become steadily more expensive. In 2008, for the first time over $1 billion was spent on the presidential election alone (with Barack Obama raising an unprecedented $635 million). With all the other elections, to Congress and for political office at state and local level, taking place at the same time, an estimated $5.7 billion was spent on political campaigning in 2007–08.

A range of factors is driving up the cost of campaigning:
- The increasing sophistication and professionalism of campaign teams has made campaigns more expensive.

- In presidential campaigns, an increasing number of primaries are held early in the year (a process known as 'front-loading'), which means that candidates have to raise substantial funds before the process begins.
- This in turn has led to the development of the 'invisible primary', a period before the primaries and caucuses begin when likely candidates have to prove that they have sufficient name recognition and fundraising capacity to sustain a long and gruelling presidential election campaign.

These costs have led to fears that candidates become more concerned with the interests of wealthy donors who fund their campaigns than with the interests of the voters. To address these concerns, legislation has been passed with the aim of both reducing the cost of elections and ensuring that the influence of wealthy donors is limited.

Matching funds

In the 1970s, a system of matching funds was set up for presidential campaigns. In return for candidates agreeing to limit the amount of funds they raised during the primaries, a public fund would provide them with an equal amount. In 2008, candidates could raise up to $48 million and receive an equal amount from the fund. Similarly, during the general election campaign, candidates are entitled to public funds for their campaign if they agree not to raise any money privately once the party convention is over. In 2008, this figure was $84 million.

However, candidates have demonstrated in recent elections that they are able to raise more than the amount they could receive from such funds and, increasingly, accepting matching funds is seen as a sign of weakness — evidence that the candidate is not popular enough to raise the war-chest needed to compete.

In 2008, Barack Obama and Hillary Clinton had each raised over $100 million by the time the primaries began, and Barack Obama went on to add a further $200 million to his campaign funds by the end of the nomination process. Inevitably, all the other candidates, especially those who lagged behind despite accepting matching funds, appeared weak by comparison.

The 2008 presidential contest was the first time one of the candidates did not accept public financing for the general election. The Republican candidate, John McCain, had raised funds for the general election campaign before his party's national convention but accepted public financing, which meant he could not raise any more after the convention. In total, that gave him £130 million to spend. Barack Obama, by declining public funds, faced no such restrictions. He raised a record $66 million in August and then smashed that record in September with an income of more than $150 million, giving him well over $200 million to spend in the final month of the campaign.

Campaign finance

The main source of the vast sums of money required is rich organised groups and individuals, and campaign donations are not seen as a form of charity: it is expected that there will be political benefits for the most active supporters of candidates once they take office. Hence the concern that the interests of the wealthy will outweigh those of ordinary voters once elections have taken place.

Legislation

To address this concern, legislation in the 1970s introduced mechanisms to limit the amount individuals and groups could contribute to candidates running in federal elections. These mechanisms, however, have not proved very effective. In particular, candidates and parties were allowed to accept unlimited donations if they were to be used to promote political education and participation in elections. These donations, know as 'soft money', were often abused by candidates, who used them to 'educate' the voters on their own strengths and their opponents' weaknesses and faults.

In 2002, Congress passed the Bipartisan Campaign Reform Act (BCRA), which banned candidates and political parties from accepting so-called 'soft money' campaign contributions. However, wealthy individuals and groups who did not want to see their influence diluted swiftly devised a loophole: they set up their own organisations that could campaign separately, but alongside their preferred candidate or party, as long as there was no coordination between the campaigns. Known as 527 groups, these organisations spent substantial sums in the 2004 presidential election. In 2008, however, they had no meaningful impact on the election.

Citizen donations

With so much money spent in 2008, some questioned whether this would lead to another round of campaign finance legislation to curb expenditure. In the immediate aftermath of the election, there was little pressure for such changes. In part, this was because there were so many other major issues to address, including an economy in recession and wars in Iraq and Afghanistan. However, it was also because such a high proportion of Barack Obama's record-breaking donations came from ordinary citizens contributing small sums of less than $200 each. This kind of campaign donation was widely welcomed, as it was seen as a form of active political participation that is healthy in a democracy. Ordinary people who donate, with no expectation of reward, will also vote and encourage their friends and relatives to participate politically. Also, there was no sense that Obama owed his success to any identifiable group that might expect special treatment. As long as such perceptions remain, the campaign finance system is unlikely to be reformed again.

Participation

Throughout the 1970s, 1980s and 1990s, the USA saw steadily declining participation in elections. In part, this was seen as a consequence of the nature of US society and its electoral system.

Registration

Almost one-fifth of American voters move to a new location every 5 years. Many of them may not have met the registration requirements enabling them to vote or may not have registered to vote in their new location. The 'motor voter' law of 1993 was introduced to allow voters to register when they renew, or change their address on, their driving licence, but it did not appear to have a significant impact.

The frequency, number and length of American elections lead some voters to become jaded with the process and reluctant to participate.

Exclusion

Some states limit the participation of adults who have served a prison sentence or suffered mental illness. In 13 states, a felony conviction results in disenfranchisement for life. In the 2000 presidential election, this meant that over 200,000 people in Florida alone were excluded from the electoral process, despite having 'paid their debt to society'.

Concerns

In the presidential elections of 2004 and 2008, the rate of participation increased dramatically. However, some concerns about electoral participation remain. It continues to be the case that the poorer people are, the less likely they are to believe their vote will make a difference.

The decline in participation may be due to a perception that politicians are more concerned with meeting the needs of their financial backers than the needs of voters, which makes voting pointless. It may also be due to the record of politicians who have proved unable to address effectively many of the issues of greatest concern to the poor and vulnerable in American society, such as spiralling health-care costs.

Boundaries

Finally, there is one disincentive to vote in congressional elections that affects most Americans. Modern computer programmes, combined with market research data, make it possible to draw the boundaries of congressional districts in ways that virtu-ally guarantee victory for one of the main parties. In most states, the process of drawing the boundaries is carried out by the party that controls the state legislature rather than by a neutral body. Thus boundaries may be drawn that concentrate opposi-tion supporters in just a few districts, leaving the ruling party with a comfortable majority in a larger number of districts. Effectively, the politicians are choosing their voters instead of the voters choosing their politicians. Under these circumstances, it is not surprising that participation in congressional elections is low and that few Congressmen lose elections.

Conclusion

The exam questions relating to this topic address the themes of how the US electoral system works, whether that system is effective at holding elected politicians to account, the concerns that have become the focus of political debate and the effec-tiveness of reforms that have been introduced to improve the system.

There may also be questions on the factors influencing the outcome of the most recent election.

In all cases, your analysis will be more effective if you can support it with the use of relevant examples.

Pressure groups

The Founding Fathers feared 'factions'. By this they meant any group of people who organised themselves to advance their interests at the expense of everyone else. This could include providing financial help to people running in elections, in the hope of favourable treatment if they won — as discussed in the previous section. This intense suspicion of 'special interests' is as much a feature of modern politics in the USA as it was when the Constitution was written.

Yet, for the Founding Fathers, 'the people' should ultimately be sovereign, and politicians should serve their interests. If the people are to be able to communicate their needs and wishes to those in power, between elections, they need to be organised. Thus it would seem that pressure groups are essential to the Founding Fathers' vision of an active citizenry holding its leaders accountable.

When you are analysing US pressure groups, therefore, the central theme is whether they are helpful or harmful to American democracy.

Aims of pressure groups

The term 'pressure group' is applied to a vast range of organisations with little in common. However, they all have a shared purpose: they seek to advance their own interests or to promote a cause they believe in.

Pressure groups can range from a community organising to push their local council to turn some wasteland into a baseball diamond for the young people of the area, to consortiums of aircraft builders battling to win the contract to provide the next generation of fighter jets for the US armed forces. In every case, they want to persuade people who make policy decisions, or implement those decisions, to pass and apply laws, rules and regulations that benefit their members or their cause. This may include persuading policy-makers to provide resources available to them (money, equipment, land etc.) or, if the policy-makers are unsympathetic to the pressure groups, at least to find ways of reducing the negative impact of any decisions they take.

In order to achieve these aims, a pressure group has to identify which policy-makers are most influential in terms of the issues that are most important to it. Then it has to devise strategies that will influence those policy-makers to make the best possible decisions from the group's point of view. Access to key decision-makers is therefore crucial, and a strong grasp of the political system is essential if pressure groups are to be effective.

Access points

The USA has a federal political system, in which important decisions that make a real difference to people's lives can be made on many levels. At almost all these levels there are opportunities to influence those decisions, as policy-makers are almost always elected and there are arrangements that allow access even to unelected people.

Local

For some Americans, the most important policy-makers are those chosen from within their own community. For example, for people who regard their children's education as the most important issue, the most crucial decision-makers in the country would be the members of their local school board, all of whom are elected and therefore responsive to strongly held views. The same is true of those who are deeply concerned about crime in their community. They may be able to influence the priorities of the police and the courts, as in many parts of America the local police chief and judges are elected.

State

For other Americans, the most important decision-makers may be at state level: the Governor and members of the state legislature, where the level of taxation is set and spending priorities are determined. State politicians decide which behaviours to criminalise (making prostitution legal in Nevada, assisted suicide legal in Oregon, gay marriage legal in Massachusetts etc.) and what penalties to impose, including in some cases the death penalty.

Ballot initiatives

For individuals or groups disagreeing with decisions taken at state level, there may be the opportunity to overrule them in ballot initiatives. When elections are held, most states have a procedure whereby active citizens can have a question added to the ballot paper on almost any issue, which provides another opportunity for pressure groups to achieve their aims. In 2008, for example, the voters in California were asked whether they wanted to overturn a ruling by the state Supreme Court that permitted gay marriage. This ballot initiative, Proposition 8, drew as much public attention as the presidential election (bearing in mind that California was a rock-solid Democratic state), with over $80 million spent by supporters and opponents of the initiative. By a small margin, the proposition passed. The conflict continued, however. Californian gay-rights groups identified the Mormon church, a religious group whose members make up a majority of the population in nearby Utah, as a major force in the campaign to end gay marriage and responded with their own internet-based campaign to boycott Utah's lucrative tourism industry.

National

For yet other groups, the federal government in Washington, DC makes the most important political decisions. At this level, it is also possible for decision-makers to overturn policies made at state or local level.

Approaches

With such an array of potentially important access points to the people and bodies making key decisions, pressure groups are faced with a choice:
- seek to approach one access point, usually the one that has most influence on decisions that matter most to the pressure group, or
- seek to approach several access points, including those with the capacity to overrule the initial decision-makers and those who are responsible for implementing political decisions

Clearly, the second approach leaves less to chance. However, influencing decision-makers at different levels, with different procedures and priorities, can be a major challenge, best met by groups with many members and a substantial budget at their disposal. This may explain why prominent US pressure groups tend to be both large and wealthy, and the emergence of such groups has caused concern that they distort the democratic system, shaping laws and capturing resources in ways that are not in the best interests of the majority of the population. This issue is examined in more detail below, but first we will consider the reasons for seeking individual access at the federal level, and how it is done.

Influencing the federal government

Your course does not examine politics at local and state level in great depth, so you would not be expected to analyse how and why pressure groups seek to influence specific access points at these levels. However, you are expected to have this level of understanding in relation to the three branches of government in the nation's capital city.

The executive

One branch of government, the executive, is mainly responsible for proposing new laws and implementing those that have been passed. Does it make sense for pressure groups to focus on this branch, and if so, how do they go about it?

From the point of view of pressure groups, the executive consists of two parts that may yield distinctly different benefits if effectively influenced.

The president and his advisers work out of the White House. When the president delivers the State of the Union address each January, he shapes the political agenda for the year. This is reinforced the following week, when he sends his budget proposals for the year to Congress. Any pressure group that can influence this agenda is in an advantageous position. How may this level of access to the president be achieved?

Almost certainly, the group's goals will coincide with those of the president. For example, the left-leaning African-American civil rights organisation, the NAACP, was more welcome in the Clinton White House than during the presidency of George W. Bush. Conversely, the leaders of the right-wing group Progress for America had easy access to the Bush administration's officials.

Strategies

Apart from shared goals, what strategies are used by pressure groups to influence the president and his advisers?

They can demonstrate their usefulness to the president's team in a range of ways, including:

- financial contributions
- delivery of a large number of campaign activists and the votes of a large number of their supporters
- provision of expertise in policy areas on the president's agenda
- public support for the president's political priorities

Iron triangles

For those without access to the White House, all is not lost. If the president is able to get his policies turned into law by Congress (where opponents will do their best to block them), they then have to be implemented by the government departments that make up the federal bureaucracy. The civil servants who work in these departments may have long-term projects that do not have the support of the president and may be willing to work with groups who support their priorities. If these two groups are joined by key members of congressional committees, which fund the work of the executive branch, an 'iron triangle' is formed, which can implement programmes in ways that thwart the will of the president.

The legislature

Another branch of government, the legislature, is mainly responsible for passing new laws and scrutinising the work of the executive, especially in relation to appointments to high office and foreign policy. Does it make sense for pressure groups to focus on this branch, and if so, how do they go about it?

From the point of view of pressure groups, the legislature also consists of two distinct parts: the House of Representatives and the Senate. In some cases, it is essential to influence both in order for groups to achieve their goals, but on other occasions one of the two chambers of Congress may be more significant than the other.

Bills

Pressure groups want to influence Congress as a whole if they support the passage of specific legislation. A bill can only become law if it is passed, in identical form, by both the House of Representatives and the Senate. However, achieving this goal is a tremendous challenge. A bill can face various challenges before it is passed:

Figure 1 The iron triangle

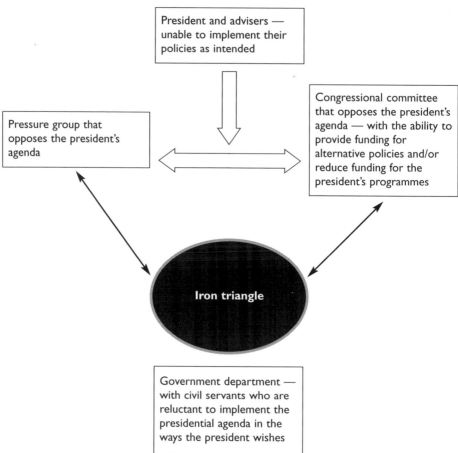

- **A divided Congress.** The party in the majority in one chamber of Congress may not be in control of the other chamber. Any bill that does not have the support of both parties is unlikely to succeed in these circumstances.
- **Committee chairmen.** Bills that do not have the support of these influential figures are unlikely to succeed.
- **Filibusters.** In the Senate, the procedure known as the filibuster can be used to block the progress of any measure. A filibuster can be overcome with a special vote, called a cloture, but this requires the support of 60 Senators (out of 100), which means that even if one of the parties is united in support of the measure it may not succeed, as it is unusual for one party to have more than 60% of Senate seats.

For pressure groups, therefore, it is often more productive to persuade members of Congress to insert a helpful provision into a bill or to convince sympathetic members to block legislation that the group opposes than to put their weight behind an entire bill.

House of Representatives

In the case of the House of Representatives, the provisions that usually matter most to pressure groups are those concerning money. Constitutionally, the House is the first to consider any legislation that involves the raising of taxes (called ways and means) or the spending of public funds (called appropriations). Although the Senate may later offer alternative suggestions, it is the House that takes the lead in deciding whether to impose or abolish taxes or to raise or lower the level of tax — all of which is likely to be of interest to pressure groups. Similarly, the House shapes the debate on the priorities for spending America's $1.7 trillion annual budget. Securing even a tiny slice of such vast sums could make a big difference to many pressure groups.

Senate

For some pressure groups, other congressional powers rival money in importance, especially in respect of the exclusive powers of the Senate. This chamber has responsibility for two key areas of government.

Foreign policy issues

Any treaty negotiated by the president and his team at the State Department has to be ratified by a two-thirds majority of the Senate. This means that any group opposing a treaty that has been signed by the USA can stop it coming into force if it can persuade just 34 Senators to oppose it. Thus, when President Clinton signed the Kyoto protocol on climate change, industry groups combined to persuade so many Senators that it was not in the country's best interests that he did not even present it to the Senate for ratification.

Confirming significant appointments

Appointments of people to run government departments (members of the cabinet), ambassadors, senior officers in the armed forces and, most importantly, judges in the federal courts have to be confirmed by the Senate. In each case, it takes a simple majority (more than half) for the appointment to be confirmed. Pressure groups that feel strongly about proposed appointments will do their best to persuade Senators to support or oppose the nomination. When President George W. Bush nominated Harriet Miers as a Supreme Court justice in 2005 to replace a retiring female judge, social conservative pressure groups concerned that she did not fully share their views mounted a strong campaign against her, both publicly and behind the scenes, until her nomination was withdrawn. Instead, Samuel Alito was nominated and confirmed by the conservative majority in the Senate.

Strategies

What strategies are used by pressure groups to influence members of the House of Representatives and the Senate?

Wealthy pressure groups are likely to have a team of professional lobbyists whose full-time occupation is to influence policy-makers. They aim to build a relationship with members of Congress and their staff through regular direct contact. Lobbyists aim to be seen as supporting the work of Congressmen and Senators, to the benefit of constituents, as well as advancing the interests of the pressure groups. To these ends, lobbyists pursue a number of activities:

- **Establishing close ties with people working in Congress.** Often they are able to do so as a result of the 'revolving door' syndrome, as many lobbyists are former legislators, bureaucrats, presidential advisers and assistants with extensive contacts in Congress.
- **Providing useful information and expertise.** For policy-makers to make their mark, the advice of experienced former policy-makers and the resources of their organisation can be invaluable. Alternatively, lobbyists are often used to testify as experts before congressional committees.
- **Offering grass-roots support.** Lobbyists for organisations with a mass member- ship may use the promise of mobilising their members in support of an elected official in return for support on issues of importance to them.
- **Securing financial support.** Lobbyists for wealthy organisations may use the promise of financial support during election campaigns in return for support on issues of importance to them.
- **Mounting publicity campaigns.** Lobbyists may use their pressure group's resources to help members of Congress to generate support for proposals through their links with important people who can contribute articles to influential newspa- pers. Similarly, during Senate confirmation hearings, pressure groups may mount campaigns for or against a nominee to help Senators to justify their vote for or against the nominee.

The judiciary

The third branch of government, the federal judiciary, has the power to determine what the Constitution means and how it is applied in this day and age. Does it make sense for pressure groups to focus on this branch and, given that its members are not elected, how do they go about it?

The federal courts are potentially the most important branch of government because, in practice, the US Constitution means whatever the Supreme Court says it means. Therefore, if a pressure group successfully influences the court to adopt its views, all laws and government policies have to be based on the court's ruling. For example, since the *Roe v Wade* judgement in 1973, it has not been possible to prevent a woman from choosing to terminate her pregnancy if she so wishes.

Persuading the Supreme Court to rule in their favour is desirable for all pressure groups, but is particularly important to minority groups. Often they do not have the resources or level of support in the White House or Congress to exert influence over the laws that are passed or the distribution of federal funds. If they can afford an effective legal team, however, they can have a substantial impact on US politics.

Strategies

What strategies are used by pressure groups to influence judges?

First, pressure groups are more likely to be able to persuade judges to rule in their favour if sympathetic judges are nominated whenever there is a vacancy. This has become increasingly important in recent years as life expectancy increases and judges remain on the bench for up to 30 years. Pressure groups will therefore combine resources with each other to mount the most effective campaign possible, either in support of or in opposition to a candidate, using them to:
- compile detailed dossiers on the nominee to highlight their strengths (if the groups support them) or weaknesses (if they oppose them)
- encourage their members to join the campaign by contacting their Senators and adding to the pressure for their elected representatives to vote in line with the pressure groups' views
- publicise their support or opposition through newspapers and television in order to build wider public support for their campaign
- mount demonstrations during the confirmation hearings
- brief their allies in the Senate on the most challenging questions to put to the nominee they oppose during the hearings
- coach their favoured nominee on how to answer difficult questions

In 1987, a liberal pressure group, People for the American Way, led an aggressive campaign against an extremely conservative nominee to the Supreme Court, Robert Bork, which contributed to him not being confirmed.

Rulings

Regardless of the composition of the Supreme Court, pressure groups always attempt to influence rulings on high-profile, controversial issues. They do this in various ways:
- **Bringing test cases to court.** For example, in 1954 the NAACP won the case of *Brown v Board of Education, Topeka, Kansas*, which outlawed racial segregation. This case may have had a greater impact on US society than any other pressure-group initiative in the twentieth century.
- **Submitting amicus briefs.** The federal courts in the USA allow pressure groups to make contributions to cases in which they do not play a direct role but which have an impact on issues that concern them. These have been known to influence the court's decisions. For example, in a 2003 case on affirmative action, *Grutter v Bollinger*, over 350 amicus briefs were submitted and the verdict made reference to their influence.
- **Influencing the climate of legal opinion.** Lawyers working for pressure groups submit articles to scholarly legal journals, arguing in favour of the causes they support.

Summary of pressure groups and access points

Access point	Main methods	Intended outcomes
Elected providers of local services (local council, school boards, senior police officers, judges etc.)	Persuade sympathetic local people to run for office or actively campaign for candidates who support the group's aims	Policies that the group supports are adopted and resources are allocated in ways the group approves of
Elected state politicians (Governor, members of the state legislature, senior judges in states where they are elected)	Provide campaign funds for candidates the group approves of; encourage group members to join the campaign and to vote	Policy is made by sympathetic politicians
	After election, lobby those in office to propose laws (Governor), to pass them (legislature) and to implement them in ways the group approves of (Governor)	Sympathetic politicians are aware of the group's views on all the issues they have to deal with, and the opposition of unsympathetic politicians is weakened
State ballot initiatives	Provide funds to employ people to collect the number of signatures needed to get a measure added to the ballot	Policies that are not supported by elected politicians are adopted
	Fund the campaign, especially television and radio advertising, to ensure the measure attracts support and is passed	
The executive branch of the federal government	Provide campaign funds for a candidate the group approves of; encourage group members to join the campaign and to vote	An ally is elected to the nation's highest office; influence over a grateful president's political agenda
	After election, lobby those in the White House to propose laws and to work with the federal bureaucracy to ensure they are implemented as intended	Ability to help implement the presidential agenda
	Alternatively, if they oppose the president's policies, they may seek to work with civil servants and congressional committees who share their views to resist implementation of the policies	Ability to block the implementation of the president's agenda

Access point	Main methods	Intended outcomes
The House of Representatives	Provide campaign funds for candidates the group approves of; encourage group members to join the campaigns and to vote After election, lobby Congressmen to pass bills the group supports, especially those that will result in funds/resources that will aid the group's members or cause	Allies elected to the body with primary responsibility for the nation's $1.7 trillion budget
The Senate	Provide campaign funds for candidates the group approves of; encourage group members to join the campaigns and to vote After election, lobby Senators to pass bills the group supports or to persuade them to block legislation that the group opposes, using a filibuster if necessary (when opponents do not have a majority in either house of Congress)	Allies elected to an assembly with the ability to pass federal laws or to block legislation that may have the support of the majority party Allies appointed to key positions in the executive branch or, even more importantly, in the judicial branch
	Lobby sympathetic Senators on votes confirming presidential appointments and ratifying treaties Mount campaigns encouraging the public to put pressure on unsympathetic Senators in votes on confirming presidential appointments and ratifying treaties	Appointment of opponents to key positions in the executive branch or, even more importantly, the judicial branch, blocked
The federal judiciary (especially the Supreme Court)	Campaign for or against nominees to federal courts Identify promising test cases on issues important to the group and provide legal expertise and funding to take them through the court system Prepare amicus briefs on cases of significance to the group	Allies appointed to the judicial branch and opponents blocked Federal judges provided with an opportunity to interpret the Constitution in ways that benefit the group's members or cause Judges interpret the Constitution in ways that benefit the group's members or cause

Regulating pressure groups

The Founding Fathers' concern that 'factions' might use access points to advance their interests at the expense of the wider population has been shared by subsequent observers of the US political process. Politicians have periodically found themselves under pressure to ensure that the activities of pressure groups are closely monitored and, in some respects, regulated.

As we have seen, the ability of pressure groups to influence elections through financial contributions has been subjected to campaign finance regulations.

Initiatives

The ability of pressure groups to influence policy-makers at local and state level is regulated by the state governments. However, when these rules are perceived to be too weak, groups that aim to promote open and accountable government (such as Common Cause or Democracy 21) may propose initiatives to tighten regulations. In 2008, for example, there were three ballot initiatives on the Colorado ballot paper to restrict the activities of lobbyists and the rights of companies seeking contracts with the state government to make financial contributions to politicians.

Legislation

The practice of lobbying the federal government is regulated by the Lobbying Disclosure Act of 1995. This restricts lobbyists acting on behalf of their groups from giving gifts (which could potentially be bribes) to members of Congress or their staff. It also restricts former legislators, their staff and members of the executive branch from working for pressure groups for at least a year after they leave their governmental posts, to prevent the appearance of a conflict of interest (being seen to have acted in the interests of the pressure group while still serving in government). After a scandal in 2006 revealing that the highly influential lobbyist Jack Abramoff had largely ignored the lobbying rules, the regulations were tightened in new legislation passed in 2007 that effectively banned all gifts.

The overall impact of pressure groups

Given the political landscape of the USA, it is not surprising that the most significant pressure groups tend to be larger and wealthier than their counterparts in other countries. Any pressure group capable of effectively exerting influence on policy-makers at the local, state and federal level is likely to have a large membership and substantial financial resources. For example, the National Rifle Association (NRA), which protects the interests of gun owners, gun retailers and gun manufacturers, has a national membership of over 4 million, organised into active local groups that can respond to state regulation of gun ownership, and an annual budget of over $150 million per year, of which at least $30 million is spent on what is regarded as the most formidable lobbying operation in the country. It is clearly no coincidence that it has proved difficult for politicians, at both state and federal level, to pass gun-control legislation (which the NRA fiercely opposes), even in the aftermath of massacres that take place periodically in the USA, such as the shooting at Columbine High School, Colorado, in 1999, when 12 students and a teacher were killed.

Is it healthy for specific interest groups to have such levels of influence in a democracy that, ideally, serves the interests of *all* Americans?

This question is at the core of all essays on pressure groups. The answer, as with so much else in politics, is that different Americans, depending on their ideological perspective, reach different conclusions.

The left

For many on the left of US politics, large, well-funded groups tend to serve the interests of the wealthier sections of society. These have the resources to set up effective organisations with well-equipped offices and well-qualified staff and, above all, to employ people who have worked in government and have detailed knowledge of its workings and extensive contacts among their former colleagues (the 'revolving door' system). With all these advantages, the left believes that these groups:
- are far more likely to influence the nature of legislation introduced, its provisions and the resources it allocates than are disadvantaged, unorganised groups such as the homeless, whose needs may be much greater
- have proved effective at evading the regulations designed to limit their influence, which is why lobbying and campaign finance rules seem always in need of strengthening
- play too large a role in elections, funding the candidates who support their cause and doing their best to ensure that the issues that matter most to them are the focus of election campaigns; as these issues are often divisive (and thus referred to as 'wedge' issues), pressure groups are perceived to divide rather than unite Americans

For those on the left, therefore, the concerns of the Founding Fathers were legitimate and they tend to be critical of the role played by pressure groups in modern America.

The right

For many on the right of US politics, the ability of all Americans to organise and make their voices heard means that the policies that emerge from vigorous debate between rival viewpoints are likely to be in the best interests of the majority. They dispute the claim that only one section of society gets its way all the time and that less privileged groups never benefit from decisions made by policy-makers. They support these arguments with the following points:
- Landmark events such as the Supreme Court's *Brown v Board* ruling in 1954, which clearly benefited a disadvantaged group, demonstrate that there are meaningful opportunities for all groups in society to influence policy.

- Pressure groups serve to engage people in the democratic process on a continuing basis, not just at elections, which is healthy in a democracy.

In response to the claim that pressure groups tend to divide Americans, supporters of their role in society point out that at local level, organised groups tend to bring different sections of communities together to work for their shared interests. They argue that at national level there are genuine differences between sections of American society, and that pressure groups are more an expression of these differences than the cause.

Conclusion

The exam questions relating to this topic address the themes of how pressure groups exert influence on policy-makers and whether their ability to do so has a positive or negative impact on democracy in the USA.

Short questions tend to focus particularly on the reasons why pressure groups target specific branches of the federal government and the methods they use. Sometimes the focus is on how effective the regulations are in limiting the impact of pressure groups.

Essays tend to examine the criticisms of the impact of pressure groups on US democracy and debates about the validity of those criticisms.

In all cases, your analysis will be more effective if you can support it with the use of relevant examples.

Political parties

The Founding Fathers' fear of 'factions' applied to political parties to an even greater degree than it did to pressure groups. While pressure groups seek to influence policy-makers to the advantage of their members or cause, political parties aim to go one step further and win power so that they can use the instruments of government to the benefit of their supporters and the issues they are committed to.

This is not necessarily a bad thing. Political parties offer the general public a range of alternative programmes for running communities or the country, they attract people with ideas and leadership skills and provide them with opportunities to present themselves to the general public, and they take responsibility for putting their ideas into practice. If the political parties fail to play this role, the voters can find it difficult to express a clear preference for a political direction in elections.

However, in countries with a 'winner takes all' electoral system, with well-organised parties pursuing an agenda that favours some sections of the population at the expense of the rest, there are grounds for a resurgence of the Founding Fathers' concern that the parties could be little more than vehicles enabling competing 'special interests' to gain control of the policy-making process and use it to their own advantage.

When you are analysing political parties, therefore, the central issues are how well organised they are, which sections of society they represent, and which direction they wish to set for the country.

Umbrella parties

For most of the nineteenth and twentieth centuries, the main political parties in most European countries were committed to one of the three broad ideologies: socialism, liberalism or conservatism.

In contrast, for lengthy periods of American history the main political parties had no similar ideological focus. Instead they were made up of loose coalitions representing different sections of the population, which often had little in common even though they supported the same party. Covering such a wide range of disparate groups, the main parties were often referred to as 'umbrella' parties.

Historical allegiance

The Democratic Party, for example, drew its support mainly from three groups of people who had historical allegiances to the party. White communities in the southern states were loyal to the Democratic Party because of its role in the Civil War. Overwhelmingly Anglo-Saxon and Protestant, these southern conservative voters were not only hostile to their black neighbours but also harboured suspicion and prejudice towards Catholics and Jews who originated from other parts of Europe. Yet in the northern cities, for example New York, Boston and Chicago, Catholics from countries such as Ireland, Italy, Poland and the Ukraine and Jews fleeing persecution in Europe were also loyal supporters of the Democratic Party for their own historical reasons.

New Deal Coalition

Then, in the 1930s, when Democratic President F. D. Roosevelt led the country through the Great Depression, two other groups were drawn into the Democratic camp: industrial workers who benefited from government-funded programmes to build schools, roads etc. and who were legally protected when they joined trade unions to secure adequate wages and working conditions, and urban African-Americans who also found jobs or received benefits that enabled them to survive the economic slump. This combination of supporters became known as the New Deal Coalition.

Left and right

Clearly, a party that represents such a wide range of people who may have conflicting interests will find it difficult to be tied to one clear ideological position.

Because of the policies of President F. D. Roosevelt, and because the urban groups within the coalition generally favoured government intervention to protect the poor and vulnerable, the Democratic Party was seen as the more left wing of the two main parties. However, with such a significant proportion of its members in the South being very right wing and its Catholic supporters being quite conservative on social issues such as the role of women in society, the Democratic Party was not at all like the socialist parties that attracted the support of the poor and vulnerable in European countries.

With the support of rural communities, the middle class and wealthy sections of society, the Republican Party tended to be seen as the more conservative of the two main parties. However, because it was shunned by the conservative South and because some of its wealthy supporters believed that the government should be supportive of poorer sections of the community, its policies were quite distinct from those of conservative parties in Europe.

Party realignment

Two developments in the 1960s sparked a trend for conservatives in the Democratic Party to shift their support to the Republicans.

Civil rights

The first such development was the Civil Rights movement. Under Democratic Presidents Kennedy and Johnson, the party threw its weight behind the campaign for equal rights for African-Americans. This put it at odds with the leading politicians in the South, also Democrats, who fiercely protected (often violently) laws and customs that asserted white racial supremacy. When President Johnson signed the Voting Rights Act in 1965, he commented that 'we have lost the South for a generation'. In fact, it took a while for the South to make the transition to the Republican Party, but in time it would appear that the Democrats had lost their support permanently.

New lifestyles

The second development was the rise of 'alternative' lifestyles. With the Democratic Party's history of being more accommodating to those who were marginalised by mainstream society, people espousing such lifestyles tended to gravitate towards it. This alarmed socially conservative supporters of the party, especially ethnic Catholics. Some of these left the party, and all of them became more receptive to Republican candidates for the presidency if they felt that the Democratic nominee was too left wing ('liberal' in US political language) on social issues.

Consequently, by the 1990s the New Deal Coalition was no longer intact, with white southerners and more conservative Catholics having left the party.

Democratic Party support

Key groups

The loss of white southerners and some ethnic Catholics left the Democratic Party with the support of the following groups:

Urban working-class white Americans

This group especially included people employed in highly unionised industries. However, they could be tempted away from the party by a Republican who appealed to them — such as Ronald Reagan in 1980, whom they saw as a stronger, more effective leader.

Very highly educated, wealthy white Americans

Many of these voters have an ideological commitment to a fairer society and support policies to achieve this goal, even if it comes at some personal cost such as higher taxes on the highest earners.

Well-educated young Americans

These are people under 30 with a university degree and, in most cases, working in professional jobs. They are liberal on social issues, and their growing support is often in reaction to the perceived intolerance of Republicans on issues such as gay rights and women's rights.

African-Americans

Since the Civil Rights movement in the 1950s and 1960s, African-Americans have been the most loyal supporters of the Democrats, with more than 90% voting for the party in every presidential election over the past 40 years (with the exception of 2004, when only 89% of black voters cast their ballot for the Democratic candidate). Even when the Democratic Party has had a white candidate running against a black Republican, as happened in the 2006 Senate race in Maryland and the same year's contest for Governor of Pennsylvania, the African-American vote has stayed loyal to the Democratic Party.

Hispanics

Americans who speak Spanish as their first language tend to vote on class lines. If they have high incomes they tend to vote Republican. However, a large majority are poor and tend to vote Democrat and, as they make up a rapidly growing proportion of the population, they are increasingly important to the party. There are three significant exceptions to Hispanics voting on class lines: they tend to vote as a block when there is a Hispanic running for office, regardless of the party the candidate is representing; they also tend to vote as a block when one party (usually the Republican Party) is perceived to be pursuing aggressive policies against illegal immigrants; and Cuban-Americans of all classes are loyal supporters of the Republican Party, which they see as taking a stronger line with the communist leaders of Cuba who caused them to flee the island.

Women

Since the rise in the 1960s of the feminist movement, which has tended to have close links to the Democratic Party, and the legalisation of abortion in the Supreme Court case of *Roe v Wade* (1973), which has the support of most leading Democrats, a majority of women have consistently voted for the Democratic Party.

Others

These include a number of small groups campaigning for equal treatment, notably gay rights and disability rights groups.

Summary of Democratic Party support (including how groups voted in the 2008 presidential election)

Group (2008 vote)	Reasons for support	Level of support
Urban working-class white Americans (60%)	Tradition Many remain in unionised trades; favour interventionist economics	If unionised, strong; otherwise, put off by liberal social policies
Very highly educated, wealthy white Americans (52%)	Ideologically committed liberals Committed to the extension of constitutional rights	Strong support for the liberal wing of the party; willing to provide substantial funding for liberal candidates
Well-educated young Americans (66%)	Liberal on social issues, perceive Republicans to be intolerant on issues such as gay rights and women's rights	Growing significantly in the first decade of the twenty-first century
African-Americans (95%)	Favour interventionist economics and affirmative action	Very strong; consistently around 90% support in elections
Hispanics (67%)	Favour interventionist economics Fear of Republican immigration policies	If poor, very strong, but diminishes as wealth grows; however, regardless of wealth, support Democrats whenever Republicans pursue policies against illegal immigrants
Women (53%)	Tend to prefer Democratic social policies to those of the Republicans, especially on abortion	Strongest among single young women; weaker among older married women
Marginal groups (89%)	Committed to the extension of constitutional rights in areas such as gay rights and disability rights	Very strong; willing to provide substantial funding for liberal candidates openly supportive of their causes

Republican Party support

Key groups

Realignment has meant that the following groups now support the Republican Party:

White southern voters

Many of these who were hostile to the Civil Rights movement remain hostile to affirmative action and tend to see any measures to promote equality of opportunity as part of a general trend to undermine the position of white, heterosexual men in society.

White middle-class professionals

These often hold managerial positions at work and live in suburban areas. Concerned with excessive taxation that depresses their standard of living and government regulations that affect how they manage their organisations, they prefer a political party that has long been associated with low taxation and limited government intervention.

People making their living from nature

This group includes farmers, loggers and fishermen. Although many of these people, especially farmers, benefit from substantial government support (especially when

Summary of Republican Party support (including how groups voted in the 2008 presidential election)

Group (2008 vote)	Reasons for support	Level of support
White southerners (76%)	Hostile to affirmative action and other measures to promote equality of opportunity associated with the Democratic Party	Very strong
Suburban professionals (50%)	Favour low tax, minimal government regulation	Usually strong, but declining with the Republican Party's growing association with government intervention that appears to dictate lifestyles
Rural voters (57%)	Favour low tax and minimal government regulation, such as gun control; often socially conservative	Very strong
Social conservatives (67%)	Favour policies that improve the moral fabric of the nation — notably anti-abortion and opposed to gay rights	Very strong, with the ability to attract conservative Democrats to the Republican camp

nature treats them badly), they also tend to see government as interfering in terms of taxation and regulation. Mainly law-abiding and often needing guns in their work, they are particularly hostile to gun-control legislation that is far more likely to be sponsored by Democrats than by Republicans. Overwhelmingly white, they are also loyal to the party that is associated with encouraging people to be self-reliant.

Social conservatives

Concerned with what it sees as the declining moral health of the nation, this group wants political leaders to set a positive personal example and to pass laws that it sees as consistent with traditional Christian principles. Many of the Republican-supporting groups identified above (southerners, suburbanites, farmers) are social conservatives, and the states in the South and Midwest where they form a majority of voters are referred to as the 'Bible belt'. However, these issues have increasingly attracted the support of ethnic Catholics in and around the big cities traditionally considered loyal to the Democrats, such as Pittsburgh and Cincinnati.

Party policies

With most conservative Democrats (southerners and the most committed Catholics) having left the party since the 1960s, it is no longer as valid as it once was to describe the two main parties as 'umbrella' parties.

The addition of more conservatives to an already conservative Republican Party has made it a more distinctively right-wing party. Similarly, the loss of conservatives from the Democratic Party has resulted in it becoming more left wing.

However, despite both parties having developed clearer ideological identities, they continue to include competing views on the best way forward. What are these views and how influential are they within each party?

Democratic Party policies

There are three main organised groups within the Democratic Party.

Blue Dog Democrats

This is the most conservative faction within the party. Its members argue that Americans have become increasingly conservative and that Democrats have to respond to this trend by presenting an agenda which protects the interests of the vulnerable while respecting traditional Christian values and keeping taxes low. This agenda enables them to work with Republican moderates, and they are the least likely to vote on party lines of any identifiable group in Congress. Criticised by other members of their own party as 'Republican lite', the group had 44 members in the 110th Congress, following the 2006 mid-term election, an increase of seven compared to the previous election, and further increased its strength after the 2008 elections to 49 members of Congress.

The Democratic Leadership Council

This faction, founded in 1985, also seeks to establish a political agenda for the Democratic Party which appeals to the conservative heartland of the USA, although it is less conservative than the Blue Dog faction. The group is often identified with Bill Clinton, who became its leader in 1990 and went on to become president 2 years later. He argued that the Democrats had not been trusted by middle-class voters 'to defend our national interests abroad, to put their values into social policies at home, or to take their taxes and spend it with discipline'.

The left

This group is made up of a loose coalition of party activists and internet-based organisations on the fringes of the party, such as MoveOn.org. In the early years of the twenty-first century, they adopted a stance of no compromise with conservatives and argued that the way for the Democratic Party to win power was by fighting every conservative policy which threatened hard-won rights such as abortion, civil rights for racial minorities, gay rights etc. The growing influence of this movement was demonstrated by the defeat of Senator Lieberman in the Democratic primary ahead of the 2006 mid-term elections and, arguably, the victory of Barack Obama in the primary campaign of 2007–08 against Hillary Clinton, who was associated with the Democratic Leadership Council.

With the success of both the left and the Blue Dogs in recent elections, it is difficult to identify which is in the ascendant. One of the challenges facing students as the presidency of Barack Obama unfolds is to recognise the ideological tilts of his policies.

Republican Party policies

Three distinct strands of opinion dominate the modern Republican Party.

Social conservatives

After the 2004 presidential election, it appeared that this faction had established a position of dominance in the party. Over 22% of voters gave 'moral values' as their main motivation for voting in that election, meaning that they were motivated by concern about issues such as abortion, gay rights, school prayer and immorality in the media. An overwhelming majority of this category of voters backed President Bush, and they were credited with being the most important factor in his victory. Just 4 years later, however, their standard-bearer in the presidential campaign, vice-presidential candidate Sarah Palin, appeared to alienate moderate voters and contribute to the party's defeat.

Fiscal conservatives

This faction places tax cuts and a balanced budget at the top of its agenda. Achieving these goals implies massive cuts in government spending. Fiscal conservatives would like to see many welfare programmes reduced or eliminated, and they would like to see the federal government withdraw from policy areas traditionally administered by the states, such as education. They have been very influential in the party. For example, a fiscal conservative policy was the centrepiece of President George W. Bush's second term. He committed himself to reforming the social security system in ways that would transfer responsibility for pensions from the government to individuals. This policy had long been advocated by fiscal conservatives as an important first step in reducing the scale and scope of government and encouraging individual citizens to take responsibility for their own welfare. Like the social conservatives, however, this faction had a difficult 2008. Shortly before the presidential election, a crisis in the banking sector saw a Republican president add to the national debt with a massive bailout (over $6 trillion) of institutions that had been imperilled by their own corporate decisions — directly the opposite of how fiscal conservatives believed governments should behave.

Moderate conservatives

Organised under the banner of the Main Street Partnership, this faction was once the most important force in the Republican Party. It has tended to focus on promoting the conditions in which enterprising people can create wealth, but has also believed that the wealthy have an obligation to care for the less fortunate in society — accepting that they will have to fund welfare programmes through significant levels of tax. However, since Ronald Reagan inspired a new wave of young Americans to join the party with his campaign against 'excessive' government and church groups started encouraging their members to join the crusade against immorality, the moderate faction in the Republican Party has seen its influence decline, as the 'base' of the party (which campaigns in elections and contributes funds) has given its support to the other factions. The weakness of this faction was demonstrated in the 2008 presidential elections. Although John McCain, a leading member of the Main Street Partnership, won the Republican Party's nomination for president, he had great difficulty raising money from the party's traditional backers and generating enthusiasm from the party's membership until he started adopting policy positions of the other two factions and chose a social conservative as his running mate. Only then did the number of volunteers rise rapidly and the public see enthusiastic, boisterous support at his campaign rallies, illustrating how few grass-roots moderates were left in the Republican Party.

In the aftermath of a major election defeat, the rival factions in the losing party invariably blame each other for the result and argue that the party would have fared better if their policies had been adopted. One of the challenges in advance of the next presidential election is to track the debates within the party and recognise which faction is winning the fight for the heart and soul of the membership.

Minor parties

Where do the battles between, and within, the two main parties leave smaller parties?

Lack of success

Minor parties have never been able to attract enough support to make a substantial impact on national politics, except as 'spoilers'. A range of factors has contributed to their lack of electoral success and consequent lack of political significance:

- **The first-past-the-post electoral system.** In all countries where this system is used (including the UK), it tends to produce two dominant parties. The use of the Electoral College, which is a state-by-state winner-takes-all contest, in presidential elections adds an additional hurdle for minor parties, as it is highly unlikely that they will win even one state, much less a majority in the college.
- **Ballot rules.** These may prevent minor party candidates from putting themselves forward for election. Many states have electoral regulations designed to make it difficult for minor party candidates to be included on the ballot. Unless they have done well in a previous election, candidates have to submit signatures to demonstrate that they have significant levels of support (the number of signatures required varying from state to state). This may have the effect of absorbing most of the electoral resources of minor parties and leave little time for campaigning.
- **Federal electoral funds.** The rules governing funds to help free candidates from dependence on campaign donations work to the disadvantage of minor parties. Some funds are available to the official candidates of parties which gained over 5% of the vote in the previous presidential election. Full funding is only available to parties which gained over 25%, and even then the major parties raise substantial additional funding. In 2008, the most successful minor party candidate raised $4 million, while John McCain of the Republican Party received over $84 million in federal funds alone.
- **'Straight-ticket' voting.** This is a device that stops many people voting for minor parties. Ballot papers are often extremely complicated, with candidates standing for a wide range of posts at federal, state and local level. Many states provide voters with the opportunity to cast just one vote, for the party of their choice, for all the posts being contested. This works to the disadvantage of minor parties, as they may not have candidates for all posts and, on average, they receive twice as many votes in districts that do not allow straight-ticket voting as they do in those which provide this option.
- **Campaign costs.** Campaigns are becoming steadily more sophisticated and expensive, and minor parties often have limited funds and expertise at their disposal.
- **Sponge parties.** If a minor party produces a policy that attracts support, it is likely to be absorbed by either or both major parties, which nullifies its electoral benefit.

Impact

Despite these obstacles, third-party candidates have had some impact in recent times.

Ross Perot

In the 1992 presidential campaign, multi-billionaire Ross Perot campaigned on the failure of the main parties to tackle the budget deficit and won 18.9% of the vote. Although he secured no Electoral College votes, he drew votes away from the Republican candidate, President George H. W. Bush, which was a significant factor in the election of Bill Clinton.

Also, both of the main parties adopted Perot's deficit-reduction measures, and by the end of Bill Clinton's presidency the USA had a budget surplus for the first time in decades.

Ralph Nader

If the presence of a minor party candidate on the ballot helped the Democrats in 1992, the reverse was true in the 2000 election campaign. Ralph Nader, representing the Green Party, won just 2.7% of the vote. However, he drew votes away from the Democratic Party candidate, Al Gore. Crucially, Nader won more than 97,000 votes in Florida, a state that George W. Bush won by just 537 votes — giving him the 25 Electoral College votes which determined which of the two men became president.

Conclusion

The exam questions relating to this topic focus on the nature of the US party system. This means you have to be clear about the extent to which the two main parties are similar to, or distinctly different from, each other.

This in turn means you must have a clear view of what each party stands for, and since there are always rival factions seeking to gain ascendancy within each party you also have to know how influential those factions are at any time. This makes the use of relevant examples in your answers on this topic even more important than it is for other topics.

There may also be questions asking which sections of the population support each party and why the minor parties are of such limited significance in US politics.

Racial and ethnic politics

When they produced the Constitution, the Founding Fathers aimed to create a political system that put into practice the values expressed in the Declaration of Independence: that simply by virtue of being human beings, all people share the same core rights, the most important of which are liberty and equality of opportunity. Yet the final document they produced maintained slavery and explicitly excluded Native Americans from the 'blessings of liberty'. Two centuries later, social and political conflict arising from racial inequality is one of the most significant political issues in the USA.

Is racial inequality in the modern era the result of the system that the Founding Fathers put in place?

Many Americans think so, and believe that the USA cannot justifiably claim its political system promotes liberty and opportunity until that same system resolves the problems of racial inequality it has created.

Other Americans question the extent to which racial inequality can be blamed on the political system and, in any event, believe that it is up to individuals and communities, not politicians, to overcome such challenges.

Almost all agree, however, that the nature of racial inequality and its causes and solutions reflect the extent to which their country has actually provided opportunity for all in the past and offers genuine hope for all now. Consequently, it is one of the most passionately debated issues in US politics.

Racial inequality in the USA

Using the commonly accepted benchmarks, e.g. average income and average life expectancy, some racial and ethnic groups in the USA have enjoyed far more success than others. For example, of the 44 presidents, all but two have been white Protestant men (meaning they trace their origins to northern Europe, where the original white settlers came from). The same is true of senior executives in America's top 500 companies: in 2008, 495 of the chief operating officers of these companies were white (and 490 were men).

Immigrant communities

The descendants of immigrants from other parts of Europe (Irish, Italians, Poles, Jews etc.) who arrived in the nineteenth century have done less well. Encountering prejudice and discrimination on their arrival, they were largely confined to particular areas of the large cities and to specific manufacturing trades for several generations. It was only during the Second World War and its immediate aftermath that these groups began to routinely mix with other sections of society, find work in other sectors of the economy, improve their circumstances and move from their inner-city enclaves to the suburbs. Many continue to work in the declining manufacturing industries, such as steel production, or in the emergency services, and have not benefited from the general economic trend towards high-tech service industries.

Jim Crow

African-Americans have faced a different set of challenges. Although there have been black Americans since 1619, they were brought to the country as slaves, and after emancipation they continued to face legal restrictions on where they could live and what they could do — a system of legalised racial segregation under regulations often referred to as 'Jim Crow laws'. Designed to guarantee white racial supremacy, these laws made it impossible for most African-Americans to make the most of their talents and abilities and thereby to improve their circumstances to the benefit of themselves and their families.

Under these circumstances, with white Americans (even those facing prejudice) able to better themselves from one generation to the next, a substantial gap in the standards of living developed over time. Even the declaration by the Supreme Court in 1954 that racial segregation was unconstitutional did not lead to a narrowing of this gap, as the white communities and their political leaders in the states that had practised Jim Crow fiercely resisted racial integration. This often included the use of violence, with the result that African-Americans continued to find themselves confined to districts where basic services (education, policing etc.) received inferior funding and resources from the white authorities. Even moving to the states that did not practise Jim Crow did not necessarily make things much better. In northern cities such as New York and Detroit there was better paid work, but African-Americans were still the first to lose their jobs if their employers faced economic difficulties. African-Americans were refused skilled and managerial positions and found it almost impossible to find homes outside mainly black poverty-stricken districts such as Harlem.

Racial equality

With the election of an African-American president in 2008 and the prominence of successful black Americans in many other fields (sports, entertainment etc.), it may appear that racial inequality is no longer a problem. However, in 2008 an index of racial equality found evidence to the contrary:

- Almost a third of African-Americans were living in poverty, compared to about a tenth of white Americans.
- African-Americans were twice as likely to be unemployed as their white counter-parts.
- Just under half of all black Americans owned their own homes, compared to just over three-quarters of white Americans, and the average value of those homes was around $80,000 compared to an average value of around $124,000 for those of white Americans.
- Poorer financial circumstances led directly to a lower quality of life. African-Americans were less likely to be able to afford health insurance, which meant they were more likely to die of preventable diseases such as the many complications that arise from diabetes. In addition, with a higher percentage of African-Americans living in poor areas, they were more likely to be affected by social problems associated with deprivation, such as drug use and crime. Unsurprisingly, therefore, average life expectancy for African-Americans was 5 years less than that of white Americans.

Poverty contrasts

In 1965, when announcing the introduction of policies to address racial inequality, President Johnson argued that the nature of poverty in black communities was quite different to that in white communities. Even those white ethnic groups that had faced considerable prejudice and lived in poverty for many years 'did not have the heritage of centuries to overcome, and they did not have a cultural tradition which had been twisted and battered by endless years of hatred, nor were they excluded because of race or colour — a feeling whose dark intensity is matched by no other prejudice'.

To judge the validity of this view of racial inequality, that black disadvantage is distinctively different from that of other ethnic groups, it is necessary to examine in more detail the causes of racial inequality.

Causes of racial inequality in the USA

Slavery
The Constitution, designed to promote liberty and opportunity, permitted slavery. In a society based on the idea that all people had rights simply by virtue of being human, slavery required the denial of the humanity of those enslaved and the promotion of the idea (including convincing the slaves themselves) that they were less than fully human.

Segregation
Although the end of slavery after the American Civil War was accompanied by constitutional amendments intended to put African-Americans on the same footing as the rest of society, a crucial ruling by the Supreme Court ensured that African-Americans were not treated as equals and that the existing gap in standards of living continued to widen, even though, technically, they were free. The court judgement that ensured there would be no equal treatment in reality was *Plessy v Ferguson* (1896), which ruled that local authorities were constitutionally entitled to provided racially segregated facilities provided they were of an equal standard. As a result, African-Americans were:
- attending underfunded and poorly resourced schools
- unable to live outside areas designated for them
- denied jobs that would put them in charge of whites, effectively barring them from any skilled or managerial position
- able to receive medical treatment only at inadequate, racially segregated facilities
- denied a role in the system of law and order, including serving as police officers, as judges and on juries, with the result that justice in segregated communities was whatever the white authorities decided it was
- unable to vote, as voter registration rules were manipulated to prevent black residents from being eligible for the ballot

With a political system that denied African-Americans opportunities to improve themselves, and without the means to change the political system through democratic processes, black Americans fell further and further behind throughout the first half of the twentieth century.

Changing the law
The rules were eventually changed as a result of the Supreme Court decision that reversed *Plessy v Ferguson*. In 1954, in the case of *Brown v Board of Education*, the court ruled that racial segregation was always damaging to the minority group affected by it, thus violating the principle of equal opportunity that is a core value of the Constitution, and therefore racial segregation was unconstitutional.

However, when the southern states that practised segregation made it clear that even without a constitutional justification for their policies on race they would continue them anyway, the federal government under President Eisenhower proved reluctant to force them to change their ways. It took 11 years of civil challenge to the southern authorities, adopting the approach of non-violent resistance advocated by Dr Martin Luther King Jr, before the federal government could take decisive action to enforce the *Brown* decision and finally bring Jim Crow to an end.

In 1964, the Civil Rights Act gave the federal government the power to initiate legal action against a state, city or town to ensure equal treatment. Alternatively, the government could withhold federal funds, on which many communities were dependent. A year later, the Voting Rights Act was passed. This abolished the devices used to deny the vote to African-Americans, such as literacy tests, and prevented new devices replacing the old ones by requiring states to get clearance from the federal government before they introduced any new electoral regulations. It also gave the Department of Justice the power to send federal voter registrars to any area to ensure that no one was being denied the right to register for the vote.

Affirmative action

With the end of legalised segregation in the mid-1960s, there were no longer official barriers to progress on grounds of race. But what of the racial inequalities that had already been created and reinforced? Should anything be done to address these developments?

President Johnson argued that fairness required that the government introduce a range of policies to help African-Americans make up for the racial inequalities resulting from laws and policies that had been sanctioned under the Constitution over the previous two centuries:

> Freedom [from discriminatory laws] is not enough. You do not wipe away the scars of centuries by saying: Now you are free to go where you want, and do as you desire, and choose the leaders you please. You do not take a person who, for years, has been hobbled by chains and liberate him, bring him up to the starting line of a race and then say, 'You are free to compete with all the others' and still justly believe that you have been completely fair.

He committed his administration to provide active support for a section of the population that had been at a disadvantage because of discrimination. Collectively, such measures are known as affirmative action.

Policies

During President Johnson's presidency, affirmative action policies were introduced in two key areas: education and housing.

Education

With the statistical evidence suggesting that in areas where schools continued to be racially segregated education for black students was less well funded than that for white students, legislation was passed authorising the government to withhold funds from school districts which had failed to desegregate.

Housing

Segregation policies had created a situation in which a high proportion of African-Americans lived in sub-standard housing, so legislation was passed providing funds for more public housing (the equivalent of council homes in the UK) and allowing homes to be purchased by low-income and middle-income families in cities. Further legislation was passed banning housing discrimination, to ensure that black people would be able to move into 'white' districts.

The Philadelphia Plan

Under the next president, Richard Nixon, affirmative action received a boost in the form of the Philadelphia Plan. This required all contractors doing business with the federal government to establish 'goals and timetables' for hiring minorities and to draw up plans to demonstrate that they were taking active steps to meet their targets. In the short term this programme brought substantial benefits to African-Americans. Targeted directly at the construction industry, which previously had systematically excluded African-Americans, it directly improved job prospects for African-Americans in this sector of the economy. It also improved black employment prospects in other businesses which introduced affirmative action plans, using the Philadelphia model, to avoid similar pressure from the government.

Schools

The Supreme Court also contributed to the process of reversing the effects of past discrimination. With school desegregation making only slow progress in some parts of the country, in the case of *Swann v Charlotte-Mecklenburg* (1971) the Supreme Court not only demanded a rapid end to segregated schooling but also specified the means of achieving it — bussing of white and black children to each others' schools.

The decline of affirmative action

There was almost instant reaction against affirmative action when it was introduced in the mid-1960s. In the 1968 presidential election, Governor Wallace of Alabama, a staunch defender of white supremacy, ran as an independent and won 13.5% of the national vote, more than any other independent candidate since the Second World War, winning the states of Alabama, Arkansas, Georgia, Louisiana and Mississippi. Hostility continued to grow throughout the 1970s.

Supreme Court rulings

Towards the end of the 1970s, the Supreme Court's decisions began to reflect the public mood. In the case of *Regents of the University of California v Bakke* (1978), the court rejected the use of affirmative action as a remedy for past discrimination. Affirmative action would only be allowed if it were used to achieve 'wide exposure to the ideas and mores of students as diverse as this nation' — in short, it could be used to achieve racial and ethnic diversity in education. Even then, to achieve diversity a range of characteristics could be taken into account, of which race was an important one but not of overriding importance.

This ruling undermined the central justification of affirmative action — to correct the racial imbalances that had occurred in the past with the permission of the state's authorities, including the courts. Following this decision, the Supreme Court narrowed the scope of affirmative action programmes in other aspects of society, such as the allocation of government contracts.

In the wake of the *Bakke* ruling, affirmative action continued to be used in many areas of American life, but only to a limited extent. This was a situation that left both its supporters and its opponents dissatisfied and, ever since, both have been battling to convince the public either to extend affirmative action programmes or to have them reformed or abolished.

Arguments in favour of affirmative action

Supporters of affirmative action can be divided into two groups. Some are categorised as moderate/pragmatic (meaning practical or realistic), while others are categorised as radical (meaning favouring dramatic or thorough change).

Benefits

Moderate supporters of affirmative action emphasise ways in which American society has been improved by the programmes and the further benefits that could flow from continued or even enhanced affirmative action. They point to the following developments to support the claim that the USA has become a fairer, more integrated society as a result of affirmative action:

- **Employment.** In 1960, only 15% of African-Americans were employed in white-collar jobs such as clerical or sales positions, compared to 44% of whites. Black workers were virtually excluded from apprenticeships for skilled trades such as plumbers and electricians. By 2002, the proportion of African-Americans in white-collar jobs had risen to almost 70%.
- **Housing.** Until the 1960s, the small proportion of African-Americans who were able to build up some wealth were unable to move out of black districts into more affluent suburbs because of housing discrimination. Since the passing of the Fair Housing Act (1968), there has been a steady flow of African-Americans out of the cities into the suburbs from which they were previously excluded.

- **Education.** The percentage of African-Americans completing high school rose from 39% in 1960 to 86.8% in 2000. The number of African-Americans with a university degree was 15.5%, an increase of 43% since the 1970s.

Continuing need

Supporters of continued affirmative action argue that while these advances are to be welcomed, they are fragile and need to be built upon. They argue that affirmative action should be maintained for the following reasons:

Employment

The advances made by African-Americans in employment are precarious and, compared to the rest of the population, limited. Each time there has been an economic downturn over the past half-century, black unemployment has risen more than the national average, and when the economy has revived it has taken longer for black unemployment to come down. This, it is argued, is a pattern that public policy should address.

Housing

Home ownership is a relatively modern development among the black population, occurring at the same time as rapidly rising house prices. As a result, a dispropor-tionate number of African-American homeowners have large mortgages, many of which are 'sub-prime' loans that charge higher interest rates, absorb a high propor-tion of the family income and become unmanageable if the family suffers a financial setback. Strikingly, the economic crisis beginning in 2007 led to a disproportionate number of black families losing their homes. Meanwhile, in the inner cities, the depar-ture of professional black residents from the suburbs has led to the loss of the local taxes they paid, which in turn has meant less money for schools and services. Thus while there has been some progress in housing, the effects of past discrimination are still evident, and this too, it is argued, should be addressed by public policy.

Education

There have been improvements in education, but women have been the main benefi-ciaries: there is a case for continued action to ensure that black men also make the kind of progress that they were unable to make in the past.

The radical view

While moderates do their best to convince a sceptical public of the achievements of affirmative action and the case for maintaining it, more radical voices claim that this is not enough. The radical view is that affirmative action needs to be not just protected but extended.

White public opinion, they argue, has never accepted a concerted effort to attack black poverty and disadvantage, because the public debate on affirmative action has focused on 'fairness', meaning equal treatment of all races, ignoring the deep-seated racial *un*fairness that has developed over the past two centuries.

Corrective justice

Radicals seek to move the debate to corrective justice. This is the idea that genuine fairness can only be achieved when a deprived group has been compensated for losses, and for gains unfairly achieved by others, as a result of government action. In their view, existing affirmative action programmes have not achieved this objective, and there is no prospect of it being achieved as long as the Supreme Court upholds the *Bakke* verdict. Therefore radicals propose another approach, that the federal government should pay reparations to the African-American community for the accumulated effects of over 200 years of lost liberty and opportunity.

To achieve their goals, radicals have to convince the public that affirmative action programmes have never been proportionate to the scale of the problem they were meant to address. Arguing that the treatment meted out to African-Americans until the 1960s was on a different scale and of a different quality to the challenges faced by voluntary immigrants to the USA, they characterise slavery and Jim Crow legislation as crimes against humanity and argue that African-Americans should be compensated in a similar manner to the victims of other such crimes. They compare the plight of black Americans with that of survivors of the Jewish holocaust and descendants of its victims, Japanese-Americans who were collectively imprisoned during the Second World War as suspected enemy sympathisers, and Native Americans whose land was illegally seized in the USA and Canada. Each of these groups received apologies and financial compensation. The proposed compensation for the African-American descendants of the victims of slavery and Jim Crow legislation would not include cash payments but would ensure free healthcare and college education for black communities.

Arguments against affirmative action

Like their political rivals, opponents of affirmative action are divided on exactly what they hope to achieve and how best to secure their goals:

- Moderate opponents of affirmative action accept that there are serious levels of inequality in the USA but believe that race-conscious policies are not the best way of addressing them.
- More extreme opponents do not believe there has ever been a legitimate justification for affirmative action. Those with this viewpoint campaign for affirmative action to be declared unconstitutional and see no need for anything to replace it.

Moderate critics

Moderate opponents of affirmative action criticise it on two grounds — fairness and necessity.

Fairness

The first argument, fairness, is as follows:

- Affirmative action favours one group, on the basis of race, which is contrary to American values and the spirit of the Constitution.
- It uses one form of discrimination to compensate for another. As the old saying goes, two wrongs do not make a right.

- Affirmative action effectively forces the current generation of white Americans to compensate the current generation of black Americans for misdeeds that happened before any of them were born.

Necessity

The moderate opponents' second argument, that affirmative action may have been justified in the immediate aftermath of the Civil Rights campaigns of the 1950s and 1960s but is no longer necessary and has proved ineffective, is based on the following points:

- Since affirmative action is race-based, all members of minority communities can benefit from it, even those who have prospered and do not need help.
- Affirmative action has demonstrated that public policy cannot be used to integrate society. Although middle-class black families have moved out of the inner cities to the suburbs, white families have moved away from those areas, just as they have always done, with the result that wealthy black districts have been created.
- Public policy to help those who appear to have no meaningful hope of a better life should therefore be targeted on the most needy, of all races. Affirmative action should be income-based, to help all in poverty, and should not be race-conscious.

Hardline critics

Hardline opponents of affirmative action do not seek the reform of programmes. They want to see affirmative action completely abolished, and aim to achieve this by persuading the Supreme Court to declare it unconstitutional. This is because they see affirmative action as damaging to American society in general and to the people it aims to help in particular.

Government intervention

Hardline opponents criticise the impact of affirmative action on US society because it is based on government intervention. In contrast to the view of history outlined above, which emphasises the obstacles and denial of opportunity faced by racial minorities, opponents of affirmative action favour a view of history that stresses a relationship between progress and determination, hard work and creativity — with minimal government involvement.

From this viewpoint, government regulation and welfare are unhealthy and undermine the foundations of success. Since affirmative action involves direct government support for groups that have suffered the effects of discrimination and also involves the regulation of many areas of society (education, employment, electoral processes etc.), it is seen as damaging the economic and social model that has made the USA so successful.

Damaging impact

These disadvantages are seen as having an especially damaging impact on those groups that benefit from affirmative action, in the following ways:

- It may encourage them to be lazy. Why work hard if affirmative action programmes virtually guarantee progress?

- It may encourage them to have unrealistic expectations. For example, students who gain entry to elite colleges because of affirmative action may be ill-equipped to cope with the academic demands.
- Equally damaging is the message it sends: that the beneficiaries of affirmative action do not owe success to ability, determination and hard work but to 'preferential treatment'.

Educational gap

These arguments were given a boost in 2003 with the publication of *No Excuses* by Abigail and Stephan Thernstrom. This book, which is widely used by opponents of affirmative action, provided an in-depth study of the racial gap in educational achievement, the accuracy of which is hotly contested by their political opponents. The authors argue that people who have similar levels of educational achievement have the potential to enjoy similar standards of living. They draw the conclusion that racism is no longer a major barrier to equality of opportunity, and that public policy should be directed towards addressing unequal educational achievement. They argue that the lower standard of living of African-Americans can best be explained by poor education in black communities, which in turn is the result of the following factors:

- A higher proportion of African-American children are born into a single-parent household, to a very young mother, which does not provide a firm foundation for educational progress.
- African-American households on average contain fewer educational resources, such as books, and their children are permitted to watch far more television than children of other races.
- African-American children have a far greater tendency to misbehave at school and demonstrate less interest in learning (perhaps as a result of the two previous points).
- In contrast, other minority students, especially those originating from India and China, perform well at school even if they are from poor families and attend underresourced schools because they value education.

The conclusion the authors draw from this study is that affirmative action fails to address the true cause of the problem of racial inequality, which stems from education, not racism. The solution, logically, is to do away with affirmative action and for public policy to concentrate on raising educational standards — especially in black communities.

Conclusion

The exam questions relating to this topic focus on the political disputes about the causes of racial inequality, the extent of racial inequality in the twenty-first century, and, on the basis of these views, the strategies to reduce or eliminate racial inequality.

Americans themselves strongly disagree on each of these issues and you are not expected to find a solution. However, you are expected to demonstrate that you can explain each of the four main viewpoints on this topic and analyse the strengths and weaknesses of each argument.

Questions
&
Answers

This section of the book looks at a range of answers to the kinds of questions you may face in your Unit 3 examination. It is divided into the four content areas identified in the specification: elections and voting, pressure groups, political parties, and racial and ethnic politics.

In the case of two of these topics (elections and political parties) the sample questions have short answers, worth 15 marks. In relation to the other two topics (pressure groups and racial and ethnic politics) the sample questions are essays, worth 45 marks. All of them are accompanied by two sample answers: one of A-grade standard and the other of C-grade standard. None of the answers is intended to be perfect. Each simply represents one way of approaching the question given.

Immediately after each answer you will find some guidance on how an examiner would approach allocating marks. An overall assessment of the strengths and weaknesses of each response is given. This is followed by an explanation of how the marks would be awarded according to the three assessment objectives (AOs).

The assessment objectives are:

AO1   Demonstrate knowledge and understanding of relevant institutions, processes, political concepts, theories and debates.

AO2   Analyse and evaluate political information, arguments and explanations, and identify parallels, connections, similarities and differences between aspects of the political systems studied.

AO3   Construct and communicate coherent arguments making use of a range of appropriate political vocabulary.

- Short-answer questions:
  AO1 = 5 marks
  AO2 = 7 marks
  AO3 = 3 marks
  Total = 15 marks

- Essay questions:
  AO1 = 12 marks
  AO2 = 24 marks (includes 12 marks for synopticity)
  AO3 = 9 marks
  Total = 45 marks

Ideally, you should attempt the questions provided here without reading the answers given. Once you have done this, you can review your work in the light of the examiner's advice and comments. Remember, these answers are *not* model answers for you to learn and reproduce for the examination. It is unlikely that the questions in the examination will be worded exactly as they are here and, in any case, there is always more than one way of addressing any question.

Examiner's comments

The answers are interspersed with examiner's comments, preceded by the icon **e**. These comments identify why marks have been given and where improvements might be made.

Elections and voting

How significant are mid-term elections? (15 marks)

■ ■ ■

A-grade answer

Mid-term elections take place 2 years after presidential elections. All 435 members of the House of Representatives, except those who are retiring or have lost a primary, face re-election. The same is true of one-third of Senators, which means that either 33 or 34 states will have senatorial contests in the mid-terms.

These elections have long been seen as far less important than elections that take place in the same year as presidential elections. This is because they attract less attention. Around 40% of voters participate in mid-terms, compared to over 50% in presidential election years. Also, while people focus on national issues in presidential election years, in the mid-terms it has tended to be local factors that dominate campaigns, making it hard for political analysts to find a pattern in the results. Most importantly, there is an extremely high rate of re-election of incumbents in congressional elections, which means that in many mid-term elections there are few changes.

However, in recent years mid-term elections have appeared to grow in importance. Although participation rates remain much lower than in presidential elections, they have been climbing compared to mid-terms in the 1990s. Also, the amounts raised and spent by candidates for congressional races in mid-terms rival the amounts raised in presidential years. In the 2006 mid-terms, the average amount spent in Senate races actually exceeded the amount spent on Senate contests in 2008. The greatest change is as a result of the changing nature of mid-term elections, from local contests to national elections. Since the 1994 elections, when the Republicans captured control of Congress as a result of their 'Contract with America' campaign, most mid-terms have been fought on national issues rather than local matters. This was the case in 2002, when the Republicans expanded their representation in both houses of Congress as a result of a campaign that emphasised the importance of supporting the president in a period of national crisis, following 9/11. It was also the case in 2006, when the Democrats recaptured control of Congress as a result of a campaign that criticised the policies of President George W. Bush at a time when he was extremely unpopular, especially because of the war in Iraq.

Overall, therefore, while mid-term elections remain less significant than elections that take place in presidential election years, they are more significant than they used to be.

e This response begins with a clear demonstration that the student has a strong understanding of what is meant by 'mid-term elections' and the factors to be considered when assessing their significance. From the second paragraph, it builds an argument by outlining why mid-terms have traditionally been seen as comparatively unimportant and then explaining why they have grown in significance. By taking this approach, the response does more than simply state the factors to be taken into account (arguments for and against); it demonstrates an understanding that the importance of mid-term elections has changed over time — a feature of politics that is not always recognised by students of the subject.

Despite all these strengths, the response does have some weaknesses. The student's analysis of the growing importance of mid-term elections is more confident and detailed, using a range of examples to support the points being made, than that of the factors that led to mid-terms traditionally being seen as unimportant. While equal weight does not have to be given to rival viewpoints, it is expected that there will be some balance. Also, the student has overlooked one of the most important aspects of mid-term elections: they invariably serve to shape the strategies and tactics for the presidential election that follows 2 years later. For example, after the success of the 2002 mid-terms, the Republicans built their 2004 presidential campaign around appealing to their 'base', largely ignoring those who were not well disposed towards the president, while after their successes in the 2006 mid-terms the Democrats based their 2008 presidential campaign on the unpopularity of the Republican Party and especially that of the outgoing Republican president.

For the level of knowledge demonstrated by this response, the examiner would award 4 marks, out of 5 AO1 marks available for 'knowledge and understanding'.

For the quality of analysis, taking into account the weaknesses in the response, the examiner would award 5 marks, out of 7 AO2 marks available for 'analysing and evaluating political information'.

For the quality of the argument developed throughout the answer, the examiner would award 2 marks, out of 3 AO3 marks available for 'constructing and communicating coherent arguments'.

■ ■ ■

C-grade answer

Mid-term elections take place between presidential elections. Because they lack the profile of presidential elections, they are seen as less important. However, they have been known to have a major political impact.

The last mid-term elections took place in 2006. Despite their relatively low profile, they had a significant effect. The effects of the war in Iraq, where nearly 3,000 soldiers had been killed by the time of the election, combined with a series of scandals affecting the Republican Party (including the behaviour of a closet gay Congressman who had been an outspoken critic of gay rights) and the fierce criticisms that followed the president's handling of the flooding of New Orleans after Hurricane Katrina, led to a disastrous result for the Republican Party. It lost control of the House of Representatives and, more surprisingly, also lost control of the Senate. Immediately after the election, President George W. Bush accepted the resignations of two of the leading supporters of the war, Donald Rumsfeld and John Bolton.

Before that, the elections of 2002 also had a significant impact in a different way. Following shortly after the attacks of 9/11, the nation had given its support to the Commander-in-Chief as he responded by invading the Al-Qaeda haven in Afghanistan. So when he asked for the electorate's support by voting Republican they responded and, unusually, the president's party increased its representation in Congress in a mid-term election.

The 1998 mid-terms were more typical. There was no dramatic swing in either direction, with the Democrats making small gains. In some ways, however, this was surprising, considering the Monica Lewinsky scandal swirling around President Clinton at the time.

Probably the most significant mid-terms of recent times were in 1994. The Republicans mounted a national campaign under the banner of 'Contract with America', a radical right-wing manifesto. So successful was this campaign that it led to the Republicans seizing control of both houses of Congress for the first time in 40 years.

Overall, however, it is not easy to find a pattern in mid-term elections, which is why they are not regarded as significant.

⚡ This response is a good example of how considerable political knowledge does not always translate into a good politics exam answer. The student has provided a strong description of the past four mid-term elections. However, the answer does not build on these accounts of the elections to analyse their significance.

The fourth paragraph (beginning 'The 1998 mid-terms were more typical') suggests that the student considers mid-term elections to be of limited significance, but this viewpoint is not developed throughout the answer. In fact, as the answer progresses, the facts seem to conflict with the student's point of view, as three of the four elections cited are shown to have had a meaningful political impact.

The overall result is an answer that lacks a clear direction and fails to make best use of a substantial body of knowledge to build towards a logical conclusion.

For the level of knowledge demonstrated by this response, the examiner would award 4 marks, out of 5 AO1 marks available for 'knowledge and understanding'.

For the quality of analysis, taking into account the weaknesses in the response, the examiner would award only 3 marks, out of 7 AO2 marks available for 'analysing and evaluating political information'.

For the quality of the argument developed throughout the answer, the examiner would award only 1 mark, out of 3 AO3 marks available for 'constructing and communicating coherent arguments'.

Pressure groups

'US pressure groups are undemocratic.' Discuss.   (45 marks)

■ ■ ■

A-grade answer

Pressure groups aim to achieve their goals, to the benefit of their members or their cause, using whatever opportunities the political system provides. This would suggest that providing they operate within the law, pressure group activity is democratic. However, this essay will argue that although pressure groups make some positive contributions to the democratic process, they tend to concentrate political power and resources in the hands of already wealthy and powerful unelected groups. This is undemocratic in the sense that not all citizens have an equal opportunity to influence political decisions.

There is a variety of ways in which pressure groups in the USA can achieve their goals. However, many of these are only realistically available to groups with considerable resources.

When trying to influence Congress and the executive branch, the two best ways to gain 'access' are by having provided funds for the politician's successful election and by having effective lobbyists who may get the chance to meet senior politicians in person. If a politician owes a debt of gratitude to a pressure group, there is a greater likelihood that he or she will make political decisions to the benefit of that group. Pressure groups create this situation by providing the maximum level of funds allowed by law and encouraging their members to also make separate donations and actively work in their communities for the politician's election. (The wealthiest groups protect their interests by donating to challengers as well.) Then, after the election, they send the politician a list of their political priorities. Politicians can usually be relied upon to support the priorities of groups that contributed to their election and that can be expected to make a similar contribution when they are running for re-election. However, this may not be in the best interests of all of the voters whose interests the politicians are supposed to serve.

Similarly, when politicians or their staff leave office, they often start new careers as lobbyists, using their contacts and experience to advise Congressmen and Senators. With these advantages in high demand, only wealthy pressure groups can afford to employ them. For example, a Congressman from Louisiana was employed by the pharmaceutical industry for $2 million per year. This gives such pressure groups a great advantage when it comes to influencing new laws.

Wealthy pressure groups can also influence unelected bodies such as the judiciary. In the USA, the appointment of judges is a political decision, made by the president but subject to confirmation by the Senate. Both of these 'access points' can questions & answers

be influenced by pressure groups to secure the appointment of a judge they support or at least to block the appointment of a judge they fiercely oppose. In 1986, a Democrat-controlled Senate famously blocked the nomination of a radical right-wing judge, Robert Bork, who had been put forward by Republican President Ronald Reagan, with the left-wing pressure group, People for the American Way, playing a leading role in the campaign against him. Also, when judges are making their decisions in court, they accept *amicus curiae*, which are arguments from groups not involved in the case outlining the conclusions that they believe that judges should reach and the reasons for reaching those conclusions. Only groups with good contacts and considerable resources can hope to influence judicial appointments and employ lawyers who have the expertise to draft *amicus curiae* that are strong enough to have an effect.

In addition, many important laws are made at state or local level, making it important for groups to be able to influence politicians in each of the 50 states as well as at the federal level. Generating the resources to make a difference at so many 'access points' is out of the reach of most groups in society, giving those that can achieve this a great advantage.

Not everyone agrees that pressure groups are undemocratic. It is argued that an important feature of democracy is political participation, and in this respect pressure groups play an important role. They encourage their members to register to vote, to encourage friends and family to support candidates for office who support their causes, and to become campaign volunteers in their communities. This not only boosts participation in elections, but also serves to help educate voters.

Pressure groups are also seen as providing a means for people to remain engaged in politics between elections, by working with their group to keep the public aware of important issues, participating in letter-writing campaigns, generating support for petitions etc.

Pressure groups may help shape the political agenda, ensuring that issues which politicians consider unimportant are brought to the attention of the public, forcing the politicians to take note.

In addition, defenders of the role of pressure groups in a democracy argue that there is ample evidence of the effectiveness of groups that do not represent the powerful and influential. For example, one of the most important political developments in the twentieth century was the campaign to dismantle the system of racial segregation. The NAACP brought the landmark case of *Brown* v *Board of Education* to the Supreme Court and won, in the face of opposition from the powerful southern states. Then, public demonstrations forced the government to intervene to force local communities to end segregation. They also point to the success of the newly emerging women's movement in persuading the Supreme Court to declare abortion a constitutional right in *Roe* v *Wade*. They claim that if only pressure groups representing the wealthy were effective, these developments would never have happened.

However, although these arguments have some validity, they are weak when compared with the arguments that pressure groups are undemocratic.

While it is true that pressure groups promote political participation, people do not participate politically for the sake of it — they do so to make a difference. When there is a direct clash between the interests of well-resourced groups and less well-resourced groups, the wealthier group almost always wins. This was demonstrated by the aftermath of the Columbine Massacre in 1999. Although opinion polls found that there was overwhelming support of increased gun control after the shootings, the powerful NRA had little difficulty in blocking all gun-control measures, as they were far more organised and better resourced than the advocates of gun control. The inability of the powerless to achieving their goals may lead to them becoming disillusioned with politics and disengaging completely, which may account for the fact that there are many millions of Americans who are not even registered to vote.

Also, while there are some high-profile examples of minority groups making a major political impact, they are few and far between, which is why defenders of the role of pressure groups have to go back as far as 1954 and 1973 for their examples. Moreover, the best examples involve both the courts and street demonstrations, both of which are 'access points' used by outsider groups who find it difficult to influence the executive and legislative branches that make policy on most issues on a day-to-day basis. So these examples can be seen as evidence of the weakness of the argument that pressure groups make a positive contribution to US democracy. Influential insider groups such as the NRA do not need to take to the streets or resort to the courts to achieve their goals.

Overall, therefore, while there are examples of pressure groups playing a positive democratic role, most of the time, out of sight of ordinary Americans, pressure groups that represent the interests of the wealthiest sections of US society are doing most to shape public policy to their own advantage, which runs counter to the democratic principle of each citizen having an equal opportunity to influence political decisions.

This response seeks to make an effective argument. It begins by taking a clear stance on the question: it firmly establishes that it will attempt to support a conclusion that pressure groups are undemocratic, in the sense that democracy should provide all citizens with a meaningful opportunity to influence political decisions.

It then goes on to outline the arguments that support this conclusion, with the theme being that the most effective methods for influencing political decisions are only really available to wealthy unelected groups, effectively sidelining the majority of voters. In developing this theme, the essay is both describing how each method works *and* analysing why they tend to benefit the wealthy.

The third part of the essay examines why some political commentators believe that pressure groups, on balance, play a positive role in a democracy. This leads to the development of a counter-argument that is essential to demonstrating synoptic skills — the ability to discuss at least two viewpoints.

Finally, the essay explains why the first set of arguments outweighs the second set, thereby demonstrating the ability to evaluate viewpoints.

Overall, this approach leads to the construction of a coherent argument, a fourth skill for which the examiner awards marks.

This steady accumulation of marks for different skills, in a piece of written work that seamlessly develops a theme, is what makes this an A-grade response.

Moreover, had the response taken this approach to reach the opposite conclusion, it would have received the same grade, provided it sustained the argument as effectively. Examiners are not concerned with which conclusion candidates reach, only how well they support that conclusion.

This is not to say that this essay is perfect. It lacks examples in the paragraph that covers how pressure groups influence politicians through supporting their election campaign and how amicus briefs have been used effectively. Also, the omission of any discussion of 'iron triangles' from this part of the essay was surprising. However, an essay does not have to be perfect to achieve the highest grade.

Marks
AO1 = 9
AO2 = 10 + 10 (for synopticity)
AO3 = 8
Total = 37

■ ■ ■

C-grade answer

Pressure groups do not put up candidates for election. They do not participate in government and they do not pass laws. However, they are considered very powerful and influential in the USA. Some consider US pressure groups to be too powerful.

Power means having influence, and it is hard to deny that strong US pressure groups such as the National Rifle Association (NRA) wield significant influence. The NRA has over 3 million members and its influence is felt all over America. The NRA offers discounts to its members, lobbies against gun control and provides firearms education to schoolchildren.

In the USA, the average citizen is a member of four pressure groups, much more than the number of Americans registered to vote. More Americans are part of a pressure group than are members of a political party.

question

Only rich and popular pressure groups can 'buy' or 'hire' former Congressmen (revolving door system) to lobby for them. Pressure groups are not supposed to make or pass laws, but through their lobbying they are often able to get their own way. As they are not elected bodies with a mandate from the people, for them to be seen to shape public policy in this way can seem an assault on the democratic process.

Pressure groups can also persuade the Supreme Court. By submitting amicus briefs to the courts, they can influence crucial decisions that affect how the Constitution is interpreted. The *Roe v Wade* decision in 1973 is an example of how pressure-group power wielded by pro-choice groups led to abortion being legalised.

Pressure groups do not put up candidates for election, but the role they play in elections has almost the same effect. They support candidates by giving them money (PACs and 527 groups) for their campaigns. This power is invaluable, as successful candidates owe such groups a debt of gratitude, which may influence their voting patterns. In addition, candidates may feel an obligation to pressure groups such as the NRA, with large memberships, if they get their supporters to campaign and vote on the candidate's behalf.

The government may also respond to the ability of pressure groups to mount protests against its policies. President George W. Bush was sensitive to accusations by the black civil rights organisation, the NAACP, that his policies were having a negative effect on African-Americans.

One could also argue that pressure groups are playing an undemocratic role when government discusses its plans with an unelected body. Some pressure groups play the role of 'think tanks' for the government and for political parties, creating policy and drafting legislation for the government to use. They lack the legitimacy that comes from being elected (although it can also be argued that they provide knowledge and experience).

In conclusion, one could agree that pressure groups in the USA are 'undemocratic'. They are a force to be reckoned with, compared to their counterparts in other parts of the world, especially if they are rich and have large memberships and insider status.

✏ This essay makes a promising start. Having identified the nature of pressure groups, it indicates, by pointing out that 'some' consider pressure groups to be too powerful, that it will consider both the justifications for that view and the arguments of others who do not share that opinion.

⸱ On one level it fulfils that promise, by demonstrating considerable knowledge of how pressure groups wield influence, explaining how they operate and supporting the points made with periodic examples.

However, it fails to recognise the synoptic dimension of the essay, which requires the exploration of at least two viewpoints. Any question containing the command word 'discuss' should lead to a response that considers at least two sides of an issue. This essay considers only one — the factors that suggest that pressure groups *are* undemocratic. Thus even though this is done quite well, it could not be awarded the marks needed for the higher grades.

Marks
AO1 = 9
AO2 = 6 + 3 (for synopticity)
AO3 = 4
Total = 22

uestion 3

Political parties

What is meant by 'party renewal', and has it happened? (15 marks)

■ ■ ■

A-grade answer

The US political system used to be characterised as the main parties presenting two 'broad churches' with massive differences within them and similarities between them. The two US 'umbrella' parties both sought to represent a large, diverse nation, with the result that neither offered a clear ideological focus and they were, in essence, the same Republican Party separated by the issue of abortion. This led to David Broder's analysis that the party was 'over', with neither the Democrats nor the Republicans playing the roles expected of a political party in a liberal democracy. However, in recent years, there appears to have been an increase in political polarisation between the two parties, a process known as 'party renewal'.

Today, the Republicans and Democrats offer two clear sets of policies, providing the electorate with distinct alternatives. As they have grown apart, each has attracted the support of ideologically focused pressure groups and think-tanks pushing them away from the political centre ground, for example the National Rifle Association supporting the Republican Party and the National Organization of Women supporting the Democrats. Furthermore, moderate Republicans such as Jim Jeffords and conservative Democrats such as Zell Miller have felt that they have no place in their parties as they have become more ideologically cohesive.

There are two types of evidence of party renewal — the main ideas associated with each of the main parties and the groups who support them. The Republican Party has become increasingly associated with the ideas of the 'New Right', social and fiscal conservatism. Social conservatives are committed to ensuring that the political system encourages behaviour that is consistent with the country's core moral values, drawn from the Bible. They want to see laws passed that ban activities that they see as incompatible with the teachings of the Bible, such as abortion and homosexuality, and the government promoting activities that are consistent with Christian teachings, such as using faith-based organisations to provide welfare and education. Fiscal conservatives are committed to ensuring that government plays the minimum possible role in people's lives. (In this sense, the two most important groups within the modern Republican Party do not always agree with each other.) They believe government intervention stifles the creativity and ingenuity that made the USA the world's greatest economic power. Moreover, they object to the fact that government intervention often leads to payments for those who are not working (the unemployed) at the expense of taxes on those who are working, which acts as a disincentive for both groups to work harder. So they push for deregulation and resist any legislation that they don't see as absolutely necessary. These policies have attracted the support of white Protestants, especially men, Catholics who regularly go to church and the elderly. They are especially popular in the South and Midwest.

As these groups have become dominant in the Republican Party, the left has become dominant in the Democratic Party. Favouring government support for those who have not shared in America's prosperity and protection of those who have faced discrimination, such as racism or homophobia, this group supports government intervention and taxation of the wealthy to pay for it. These policies attract the support of ethnic minorities, people working in older manufacturing industries that may need government subsidies, and those (often well educated) who may not directly benefit from these policies but agree with them. These groups are most concentrated in the highly populated states on the two coasts, such as New York and California.

Despite these developments, there is still some overlap between the two main parties. There is a faction in the Democratic Party called the 'Blue Dogs' that is distinctly conservative and has much in common with the remaining moderates in the Republican Party, who are organised in a faction called the 'Main Street Partnership'. Also, under the leadership of President Bill Clinton, many of the policies of the Democratic Party followed the 'third way' ideas that had been developed jointly with the UK's Labour Party. By appointing many moderates and even two Republicans to his administration, President Barack Obama also took a centrist rather than a partisan approach to leadership.

In conclusion, therefore, there has been 'renewal' in the US party system but despite greater polarisation there is still overlap between the Republicans and Democrats.

This is a very good response. Sensibly, it puts the concept of 'party renewal' in context, explaining the background to recent developments. It then demonstrates the candidate's strong understanding of the issues by explaining in outline the main ideas of the two right-wing factions in the Republican Party and the left wing of the Democratic Party. (In an essay, these would have to be developed in substantially greater detail.) The candidate balances these points with an explanation of the extent to which there continues to be overlap between the main parties, and reaches a brief, logical conclusion.

However, there are time constraints on short-answer questions, and this candidate takes too long to get to the main issues of the question: they are not directly addressed until the third paragraph.

For the level of knowledge demonstrated by this response, the examiner would award 4 marks, out of 5 AO1 marks available for 'knowledge and understanding'.

For the quality of analysis, taking into account the weaknesses in the response, the examiner would award 6 marks, out of 7 AO2 marks available for 'analysing and evaluating political information'.

For the quality of the argument developed throughout the answer, the examiner would award 2 marks, out of 3 AO3 marks available for 'constructing and communicating coherent arguments'.

■ ■ ■

C-grade answer

US political parties have traditionally been seen as lacking cohesion. This is for a number of reasons. Although there are only two main parties in the USA, they have to address the needs of a wide range of people in a country that is both geographically and ethnically diverse. The interests of people in the deserts of Arizona are quite different from those in the arctic conditions of Alaska or the bustling cities of New York and Chicago. Therefore, the issues promoted by Democrats and Republicans in each of those areas will be very different to each other.

Also, there is a range of political factors that make political parties less important in the USA than in other countries. The use of primaries, when candidates are selected to represent their party, means that anyone standing for office does not necessarily have to be acceptable to the senior members of the party. This results in people holding a wide range of opinions representing the same party.

In addition, once elected, office-holders are more concerned with pleasing the 'folks back home' than with toeing the party line. This is especially true of people elected to the House of Representatives. Facing re-election every 2 years, if they encounter a situation where they have to put the interests of their districts ahead of the needs of their party, they will not hesitate to do so.

Finally, the nature of the American political system means that if the main parties adopted highly partisan positions it would be almost impossible to get anything done. One of the Founding Fathers famously described the legislative process as 'compromise, compromise, compromise'.

However, recently the parties have become more ideological. The Republican Party has attracted increasing levels of support from conservative groups that previously supported the Democrats, especially white southerners whose support for the Democratic Party was based more on historical ties (due to the Civil War) than ideology. The Democratic Party has attracted the support of more liberal voters. In the 2008 presidential election, it was notable that Barack Obama won a majority of wealthy, highly educated voters who would have been expected to vote Republican in the past but were won over by his message of inclusiveness.

Overall, therefore, there has been some party renewal, with the Democrats and Republicans both becoming more ideological, but they remain quite diverse.

In contrast to the A-grade response, this answer gets directly to the point, not using an introductory paragraph. This is good technique, as introductory paragraphs are not needed in short-answer questions. In addition, the response clearly outlines the forces which in the past have kept US political parties from becoming ideologically cohesive.

However, even in its first part the answer is at times vague and general, such as the paragraph on the need to compromise in US politics. Then in the second part, addressing the extent of party renewal, the response demonstrates little awareness of more recent developments. It shows some understanding of the changes of allegiance in some sections of the electorate but fails to demonstrate an understanding of the full scope of those changes or the reasons for them.

As a result, the response overall would get credit for demonstrating a significant amount of relevant political knowledge, but little credit for analysis and evaluation, thus barely scraping a C grade.

For the level of knowledge demonstrated by this response, the examiner would award 3 marks, out of 5 AO1 marks available for 'knowledge and understanding'.

For the quality of analysis, taking into account the weaknesses in the response, the examiner would award only 3 marks, out of 7 AO2 marks available for 'analysing and evaluating political information'.

For the quality of the argument developed throughout the answer, the examiner would award only 1 mark, out of 3 AO3 marks available for 'constructing and communicating coherent arguments'.

Racial and ethnic politics

To what extent does racism continue to be an issue in US politics? (45 marks)

■ ■ ■

A-grade answer

Some Americans believe that the effects of past racism have never been fully addressed, partly because of claims that there are continued efforts to keep racial minorities from joining mainstream society. However, other Americans believe that there are no barriers to success in US society because of race. It is the clash of these two viewpoints that makes racism a continuing issue in America.

When affirmative action was introduced in the 1960s by President Lyndon Johnson, it was based on the principle that simply getting rid of racial discrimination would be ineffective in creating a society of full and fair participation. He claimed that there had to be compensatory measures. Affirmative action is a set of programmes that aims to increase representation of a designated group or correct past and present discrimination. Supporters of this policy claim that the only way to effectively address racism is through government programmes that promote social acceptance and racial tolerance. It follows, from this point of view, that affirmative action benefits not only the designated group but society as a whole.

Moreover, racism in America is so deep-rooted that it cannot be expected to somehow evaporate. Racial discrimination was embedded in the Constitution, with freedom and equality denied to African-Americans and Native Americans. It was not until the Thirteenth, Fourteenth and Fifteenth Amendments, collectively known as the civil rights amendments, that racial discrimination was outlawed, and even after this point the southern states were allowed by the Supreme Court to set up a system of discriminatory laws. It was not until the 1954 case of *Brown v Board of Education* that this was reversed, and even then the segregation laws were only dismantled slowly in the face of violent resistance.

The events of Hurricane Katrina in 2005 illustrate how this history of racism remains relevant today. Because of the segregation laws, black residents were confined to certain vulnerable areas of New Orleans, where they continued to live. So, when the flood defences failed, it was the residents of those areas who were killed. Without affirmative action, it is argued, the past will continue to affect the present in such ways. However, with affirmative action neutralising the negative effects of past discrimination, there is a greater chance of a level playing field and equality of opportunity for all as a result.

In fact, to achieve this goal, some on the left argue that affirmative action is not enough. They argue that additional measures of providing financial reparations to African-Americans are needed for the nation to demonstrate both an understanding of the scale of the current problems inherited from the past and the scale of the national effort needed to address them.

Opponents of affirmative action reject these arguments. Partly this is because they do not accept that racism is any longer a major issue in America. There is a widespread belief that racial minorities have the same opportunities as other groups. To be realistic, those living in poor areas have fewer opportunities than those who come from wealthier districts, but this is true of all races, including whites. The fact that there are now so many successful sportsmen, actors, academics and businessmen from all races, and that the country has seen a black president elected, shows that the only real difference between Americans is ability, determination and hard work. The other reason why they reject affirmative action is that they believe that even if there is still a problem left over from the past, 'racial preferences' are not the best way to deal with them.

Some opponents of affirmative action are prepared to acknowledge that racism has been a problem in the past, especially in relation to African-Americans. However, they argue that the Civil Rights movement, together with the Civil Rights Act of 1964 and the Voting Rights Act of 1965, put an end to racist practices and that the affirmative action programmes of the 1960s and 1970s addressed the lingering effects of discrimination. Now it is no longer needed, and they see it as now having a negative impact. Because it creates the impression of preferential treatment, it has an effect opposite to what its supporters intended — increasing tension and hostility between the races instead of building bridges. Furthermore, they argue that it does not make sense to try to eliminate discrimination by practising discrimination. Therefore, any government programmes to help those who have missed out on the 'American Dream' should be based on income rather than race.

Other opponents of affirmative action, mainly on the right of US politics, adopt a much more hardline position. They do not accept that affirmative action was ever justified and would like to see the policy declared unconstitutional by the Supreme Court. They accept that racism has been, and continues to be, a feature of US society. However, they argue that this has not stopped ethnic groups from prospering in America. For example, Italian and Irish immigrants faced great hostility when they arrived in the nineteenth century, and in the latter part of the twentieth century immigrants arrived from Asian countries such as Vietnam and Korea not speaking any English, and all have made progress without government support. All other groups, according to this point of view, should be able to do the same. In addition, they see all government support programmes as creating a dependency culture that serves as a disincentive for people to work to their best.

With such strongly held, incompatible views it is inevitable that racism will continue to be a major political issue for a considerable time to come.

4
question

📝 This essay barely reaches the standard required for an A grade, not through lack of knowledge and understanding but because of the essay structure adopted. In comparison with the approach used in the A-grade essay on pressure groups (above), this essay is far less effective.

It outlines the political divide on this issue and sets out clearly the main viewpoints on each side of the debate. However, in doing so it tends to slip into description at times and to lose the thread of the argument, whereas the pressure group essay develops the case it is building throughout.

Fortunately, it manages to pick up the thread in each paragraph. Additionally, the response demonstrates good synoptic skills by recognising that although there are two main viewpoints on the significance of racism in today's America, there are differences of opinion within these viewpoints, with supporters of affirmative action disagreeing on the best way forward and the same happening with opponents of affirmative action. It is this ability to recognise a range of viewpoints on one issue that is this essay's main strength.

Marks
AO1 = 9
AO2 = 8 + 9 (for synopticity)
AO3 = 6
Total = 32

■ ■ ■

C-grade answer

There is considerable evidence of racism in modern America, but the two main parties have very different views on what to do about it.

Mandatory minimums are one area of controversy. Users of crack cocaine (usually black) have been penalised far more harshly than users of powder cocaine, who are predominantly white. This is a clear case of discrimination and of how the government treats people differently, with racist connotations.

Racial profiling is another significant problem that has been identified. Allegedly, police pursue a policy of stopping, questioning and searching people on the basis of their race or ethnicity. This has happened in Ohio, Maryland and New Jersey.

Most notably, in 2005, Hurricane Katrina revealed the effects of America's history of racism, together with its ongoing neglect of minorities. The city of New Orleans, below sea level, has long been vulnerable to floods. During the era of 'Jim Crow', as racial segregation was known, black residents were forced to live in the low-lying parts of the town, while the safer, higher areas were designated as white. Any floods were therefore going to affect African-Americans more than white Americans. Then, when Hurricane Katrina breached the flood defences, it came to light that the federal government had not maintained them to the level needed to protect the town from a Category 5 storm, which is why nearly 2,000 African-Americans died. That is why Kanye West said on national television that 'Bush doesn't care about black people'.

The two main parties have different approaches to addressing racism. The Democratic Party, through history from Roosevelt's policy of the New Deal in the 1930s onwards, has asserted the need to assist minority groups, understanding the lack of equality in America both in the past and in the present. Roosevelt's policy significantly helped African-Americans recover from the economic depression. Johnson's policy in the 1960s, the 'great society', also promoted increased rights for black Americans. Under his leadership, the Civil Right Act of 1964 was instigated by the Democrats and the party went on to propose and pass policies to help counter the effects of racial discrimination. Clinton reinforced these ties with the black community in the 1990s with positive policies to help disadvantaged minorities. As a result, the Democratic Party has regularly attracted the support of over 90% of black voters and a 2008 poll revealed that Hispanics favour the party by a margin of over 3:1.

In contrast, the Republican Party, largely supported by White Anglo-Saxons (WASPs), has opposed measures to help minorities that have experienced discrimination. Individuals who support the Republicans are likely to be wealthier than Democrats, with the Republican Party not being favoured by minorities. Because of this, it is clear that policies such as affirmative action are not in the best interests of the majority of its supporters.

Policies to correct the discriminatory policies that were in place until the 1960s have also suffered setbacks at the hands of the courts and states. In 2003, in the case of *Gratz v Bollinger*, the Supreme Court ruled that the additional points given to minorities applying to Michigan University were unconstitutional. Another example was the case of *Adarand Constructors v Pena*, when the court ruled against an affirmative action programme put forward by the government to help minority contractors. The states of California, Michigan and Washington have ruled out and banned affirmative action programmes.

In conclusion, racism continues to be a problem in the USA and the effects of past racism continue to make an impact on American society. However, with the dominance of the Republican Party in recent years, together with the attitudes demonstrated by the courts and some of the states, not a great deal has been done about it. Yet there is the prospect that political success enjoyed by the Democrats could lead to more being done.

🗨 This response demonstrates considerable knowledge of race relations in the USA and, in broad terms, the policies of the two main parties. In particular, it demonstrates a good understanding of some of the controversial issues that have highlighted racial tensions in recent years.

However, at no stage does it fully grasp the complexity of the issues, effectively reducing the political debate to one of positive, supportive Democrats against selfish, uncaring Republicans. This superficial approach was best illustrated by the treatment of the court's role. It has clearly changed over time, having previously been supportive of affirmative action, and even in 2003 the Supreme Court handed down a ruling at the same time as the *Gratz* decision that supported affirmative action. Thus, while the level of knowledge and understanding is strong, the lack of in-depth analysis limits the marks that can be awarded.

It should also be noted that sweeping statements such as 'Clinton reinforced these ties with the black community in the 1990s with positive policies to help disadvantaged minorities' cannot receive any credit unless they are explained and supported with evidence.

Marks
AO1 = 9
AO2 = 6 + 6 (for synopticity)
AO3 = 4
Total = 25

PHILIP ALLAN
UPDATES